SPIRITUAL WARFARE

by
Doreen Irvine

NOVA PUBLISHING

Nova Publishing
29 Milber Industrial Estate
Newton Abbot
Devon TQ12 4SG
ISBN 0906 330 432
© Copyright Revised edition 1992

Typeset by BP Integraphics Ltd, Bath, Avon
Printed and bound by The Bath Press Ltd, Bath, Avon

CONTENTS

FOREWORD

Over the years I have read all sorts of books and material on spiritual warfare, but it is rare to find one of this calibre. Some I have read with doubts creeping into my mind as to the validity of the contents and occasionally, complete sanity of the writers. Opinions vary from the very existence of a personal Satan through to the graphically detailed accounts of various exorcisms. Others seem to give more glory to the evil one than to God. ''What I need'' I thought, ''to complete my study, is inside information.'' After reading Doreen Irvine's book I found it.

When any country is involved in a war the best person to capture from the enemy is a high ranking officer. If he can be convinced of the utter foolishness of his leaders, of their barbarism and inability to gain eventual victory, then he may be ''turned''. His information, should it prove to be accurate, will cause untold damage to those to whom he owed his previous allegiance.

Doreen Irvine is such a person. She has come out of the enemy's camp. Her conversion from witchcraft to Christianity is a true miracle of God's mercy and grace. Her intimate knowledge of Satan's ways make this book (in the right hands), a powerful weapon against him.

No-one knows better than Doreen the fact that there is most certainly a personal Satan, although our enemy of course, would do all he can to discourage any thought of him at all. He'd prefer us to think that he doesn't exist. No-one knows better his weaknesses than someone who has for many years moved in those most evil circles.

How easy it would be to blame the fall of man on God. How simple to make it all His fault. But Doreen will have none of it! We see Satan's fall through pride and arrogance and God and His angels victorious. We find out how Satan uses truth mixed with lies to lead Christians astray. We see the truth about him in sound scriptural teaching. Set down before us is a handbook and a signpost dotted with obvious personal experiences. Doreen pulls no punches either; the church of God needs to shape up and wake up if the kingdom of darkness is going to be pushed back.

Why is it when we read the Gospels we see Jesus dealing crippling blows to the evil one and his demons, yet in contemporary Christian circles little or nothing is known about the subject of spiritual warfare? Jesus knew the reality of Satan's temptations. Did you know that approximately one third of the Gospels are taken up with this subject? He implanted into His disciples the ability to recognise the enemy, and defeat him and pass on that same message of hope. The early church followed the apostles' teaching with great joy being seen as many were set free.

Take note of the chapter on the "*Four keys of authority*" and having read it and inwardly digested, *Fear not*. When we pray, Satan trembles. When we take the keys of authority and use them he turns tail and runs. Remember James 4:7, we can only resist Satan when we are humbly in submission to our God.

This book fills the gap in my reading, may it do so for you too. As I read it, and re-read it, I was reminded once again of how great a Saviour I have. I was thrilled to find that Satan has far less power than the God I choose to serve. My Father in heaven is establishing His Kingdom on earth, is equipping His army, and the gates of hell shall not prevail against us.

Revd Andy Titmarsh
Pastor—Brook Christian Fellowship

Feb 1992

Growing, glowing, going

"**B**UT grow in the grace and knowledge of our Lord and Saviour Jesus Christ" (2 Pe 3:18). "And the end is not yet, praise the Lord". It is with these words that I ended my first book *From Witchcraft to Christ* and my second one *Set Free to Serve Christ*. So what better words to use to introduce my third book? For the end is still not yet, so much is laid up in store for those who love and serve the Lord Jesus Christ. His blessings are new every morning.

In my first book I shared something of my former way of life, and its deep involvement in the occult. By the grace and mercy of God I was delivered from that life of sheer hell, darkness and despair through the power of the risen Christ. But what has happened since then? What am I doing today? It would take far too long to write about all that has happened, but I will share briefly some of the blessing of serving the risen Christ.

Growing

I am still growing in grace, as every true Christian should, still learning more of His wonderful ways. I am now nearly sixty years old, and I do not speak at as many meetings as I once did. I have not been in the best of health over the last few years, and I have learned from this experience that it is not all important to be seen as I once was, always on the move, always travelling from one place to another. It has not been easy; but what is easy? The Christian pathway is not an easy one, and as life is changing all the time, so is our walk with God.

At first, when I became ill, I found it difficult to adjust to a quieter way of life, I was so used to being active for the Lord. Slowly, very slowly, I was able to realize that the Lord wanted to show me very important things about my future ministry and work for the Lord. I also needed rest, and rest has never come easy to me. The Lord had to show me how important rest was, and how He could use me in other ways. He showed me how to come to terms with my illness, and this gave me so much more understanding and compassion for people who suffer with poor health.

My counselling ministry, helping those who were trapped in the web of occult practices, and those affected by the occult, and Christians who were oppressed, or depressed, suddenly had to come to an end; not that I refuse to counsel, but I have to be more careful. Counselling can become very stressful, if you are not careful.

God wants us to grow in our ministry for Him, and that means wisdom in what we do and how we do it, or our ministry will be fruitless. To be tired and ill, yet persist in what you are doing is not glorifying to the Lord. How can you glow for the Lord in this state?

There have been many openings on TV and radio to speak for the Lord, and warn against occult practices, where I have been able to help people who have phoned in to ask for help, and it has been a great blessing to help people who have been afraid and lonely. I have been able to help thousands more in my TV and radio ministry than I could ever have hoped to reach by travelling, and you can reach all classes of people. There are many people that no other method can reach, such as shut-ins, who cannot get to a church service.

In my role as a counsellor it is most important to be a

good listener. If you are not a good listener, you will not be able to do the work of a counsellor, because that is the reason people want to see you. They want to pour out their heart to you. There is nothing more off-putting to someone in need, than someone interrupting every five minutes. It is also very important to be *unshockable*. If you are going to look shocked when someone tells you something that you did not quite expect, it will frighten them, and they will draw away from you. Before you begin to counsel be prepared for anything people may say, show them that nothing they say will alarm you. They will then know that you do understand.

There is joy in serving Jesus, in His word we read, "In Thy presence there is fulness of joy, at Thy right hand there are pleasures for evermore". It is my earnest desire to continue to grow in grace, and mature in my ministry, whatever that ministry may be. I want to be in the centre of God's will, and do whatever He wants me to do, and go wherever He leads.

Glowing

If we are growing in grace, we will automatically glow for the Lord. The joy of the Lord in our hearts will be seen by others, and they will be attracted to us, and we can tell them about the Saviour. People will not listen to us if our lives, and our conduct contradicts it. A warm smile can warm the coldest heart, and as children of the living God, surely we have much to smile about. There is an inner glow that will shine out to all around, showing the beauty of His grace in our hearts and lives. In times of testing "the peace that passes all understanding" will rest upon us, and in us, and this is what people want. They want peace, they want love, they want joy. When people can see that even in times of difficulty and pain, that I still have peace and victory within; this will speak to them better than my words. I like these words from a hymn written by J. G. Whittier:

Drop Thy still dews of quietness,
Till all my strivings cease.
Take from our souls the strain and stress
And let our ordered lives confess,
The beauty of Thy peace.

Christ has put a blaze of love within my heart, and this fire will continue to burn until Jesus comes or calls.

Going

As we glow we will also go. Go where? Just wherever He wants us to go, not where we think we ought to go. He alone will open doors for us, the right doors. We must always remember that we have an enemy, and he will try to stop us in every way he can. So let us be mindful of this, and pray for the right discernment, and only go through the doors that He has opened for us. We all make mistakes, and it is so easy to believe that every door opened for us is the right one. We must not forget to make things a matter for prayer before we venture forth. When we are certain the door open before us is the right door, and we are in His perfect will, He will always bless us, and give us souls for our hire. He goes before us and will guide and protect us at all times. This has been my experience in the past, and I know that this will be my experience in the future days.

I have also learned a very valuable lesson: the devil is the greatest time-waster on this earth, and he can get you running here and there, doing this and that out of the will of God. Jesus said "Follow me, and I will make you fishers of men" (Mk 1:17). If we learn to follow where He leads, and not where men want us to go, when we listen to His voice, not the voice of man He will make us a blessing to many.

I have been able to write this book because I have already taught much of it in many churches, when I have been asked to speak about spiritual warfare.

13

There is a great need in our churches for the right teaching on this very important subject. There is a need for balance on the subject of the devil, and what he is doing. Many people today are looking for direction, in a world that's going nowhere. We know where we are going—and we can point them in the right direction. Jesus said "I am the way, the truth, and the life" (Jn 14:6). We can show them the way. We can show them the truth. We cannot show them the way if we ourselves are ignorant, or if we ourselves are afraid. So let us all go forward, in faith, with a message of hope, peace, and love; with the good news of salvation. He has given us a commission to go forth in His name. Let us march forward in victory, pulling down the strongholds of the devil. Let us tread all the powers of darkness down in the power of His might. Let us all go forward for the glory of God. Let us grow, glow, and go for Jesus now, while we have the time and the opportunity.

CHAPTER ONE

Is there a devil?

IN days of old, which are often described as the "dark ages" the devil was generally believed in, and seen as a real and present force of evil. So much so, that effigies of the devil were carved in wood or stone, and displayed outside, and sometimes inside church buildings, many of which can still be seen today. I suppose this was to remind worshippers that there was a devil, and to avoid him at all costs. The devil and his demons were believed capable of almost anything, like tormenting men and women and transforming them into sinister creatures. The devil was known as "Lord of the underworld". The mood of the times was a nightmarish mixture of truth and superstition, and the greatest fear of all was to be taken over by the devil. Many people wore on their person, or displayed on their premises, amulets and charms to ward off the devil and evil spirits, to protect themselves from the prowling devil and his evil agents.

They lived in fear of the devil who was held solely responsible for many diseases, such as epilepsy, asthma, and blindness. These were reckoned to be the hallmark of the devil on a person. Everything that could not be understood, or easily explained, was put down to the work of the devil. Witches were burned at the stake, and many who were completely innocent of witchcraft were also put to death, such was the fear and the superstition of the times.

Then gradually people became more knowledgeable, and therefore more analytical and critical of their past beliefs, more scientific, and less frightened by the unseen. In reaction against their former ideas and extravagant superstition and fear, enlightened people rejected the idea of the devil altogether. To them, Satan now became just a silly word, a superstition, a figment of the imagination, a bygone fear. There was no room for the devil in modern thinking. An actual devil had no part in the new world of psychology, test-tubes, and scientific discovery. Too much was now known about sickness of the body and the mind for it to be possible to take the devil seriously, and belief in a personal devil was swept away.

The devil was now depicted in a cynical way, with horns and a spear-like tail, with a pitchfork in his hand and a wicked grin on his face. No-one could actually believe or fear such a devil. Agents of the devil, such as witches, wizards, and demons were also discarded, or better still, transformed into comic figures. For the most part the idea of a devil became a great joke.

It is the same today. Many people today still dismiss Satan as an old-fashioned comic figure from the dark ages. They just do not believe that Satan exists. Some people today think of witches as hooked-nosed old hags, riding on broomsticks over the face of the moon, or as cackling old crones stirring up a wicked brew in a bubbling cauldron. All this unbelief in the devil's existence is one of his very best camouflages. The enemy you cannot see, or believe is there, is far more powerful and dangerous than the enemy you can see, and do believe is there.

Now the modern world is beginning to think again about the reality of the devil. People are beginning to wonder if they were wrong in discarding belief in a personal devil. They are being made aware of evil in this world today, and they are searching for answers; they are asking questions about the reality of evil, and where it comes from.

Faced by evil forces that are beyond their understanding, people are slowly coming to the realisation that behind the evil conditions of this world, there must be a power, not of this world—a supernatural evil power. For despite social improvement, educational advancement, and up-to-date technology the world is becoming worse, not better.

Furthermore, there is an unhealthy fascination with occult practices, such as have never been seen before. This has been emphasised in popular books and films about the devil such as *The Exorcist*, *Rosemary's Baby*, *The Omen*, and many others. Devil-related themes are big business in Hollywood, and the paperback trade. People are emerging from the cinema, having just seen a film about the devil and demon power with a mixture of excitement, fear, and apprehension, and people can now buy video tapes about the devil, and they sit and watch them in their homes. But there is no message of warning, no word of hope, and no understanding. They are being made aware of the devil and demons without knowing the way out of it all, and the effects are sometimes alarming. This is why, back in the sixties, Christians used to stand outside cinemas trying to help those who came out, and warning those going in, pointing them to the Lord Jesus Christ, whose power is greater than the power of the devil.

There is an increasing awareness of the devil's presence, but it is still beyond most people's understanding, and worse still, they have no assurance regarding the limitation of the devil's power. The realisation that the devil does exist, with power to control or influence people, is too much for the mind to cope with, so some still hold to the callous and rigid belief that the devil does not exist, while others are stricken with great fear of the reality of the devil, and what he is doing. Both reactions are wrong.

It is easy for people, faced with the fact of increasing evil in our world, to feel that the world is on the verge of collapse, and just as the Bible states "Men will faint from terror" (Lk 21:26). Sad to say, even Christians are frequently afraid of the subject of the devil, and avoid it as something negative and unhappy. By doing so, they add to man's historical fear of the devil, and they are not

17

equipped to face and overcome the evil in this present world. They cannot help those who are in the clutches of the devil, and they cannot answer questions from those who are troubled and afraid, and are looking for a way out; they cannot help, because they themselves are afraid.

Christians should not be ignorant of the devil's devices; their eyes should be opened to the subtlety of the devil, so they are strong to fight the foe, and overcome the devil day by day. Their lives should be a shining example to those in darkness, and a testimony of victory over evil.

We can discover the cause of evil in these days from the Bible, and we can discern the pattern of demonic influence in the world today. There is no reason for Christians to be ignorant when we have an open book— the Bible, which shows us plainly the reality of a personal devil. The Bible shows us the way that the devil worked in days gone by, and the way he still works today, and it shows us how we can overcome and defeat the devil, because God is on our side. ''The one who is in you [Jesus Christ] is greater than the one who is in the world'' [the devil] (1 Jn 4:4).

Is there a devil? The question requires an honest and positive answer. What can we say to them? First of all let us consider some of the great and terrible evils that have happened in the world, and are still happening today. What, besides a personal devil, can explain how seemingly civilised, educated men, like the Nazis in World War Two could slaughter six million human beings, in a frenzied effort to wipe out the Jewish race? How, without satanic influence, can we explain the horrors of Belsen and Auschwitz, where many thousands were put to death in gas chambers? How, without a personal devil, can a man thought to be a loving father murder his children one by one, and say afterwards ''I do not know what came over me''?

How can a man who dearly loved his little girl, drug her and then throw her off a high bridge into the waters below to a certain death, because he thought the world

18

was too evil for her to live in, without a personal devil to motivate him?

One young man telephoned late one night and said, "Doreen, I have escaped from a mental hospital, because there are evil powers at work in that place, which are trying to destroy me. I have walked for hours in the rain, and I know they are still following me: I am thinking of taking my life. Can you help me?"

After talking to him for a long time on the phone, telling him of a greater power, of Jesus Christ, and how much He loved him, I tried to find out where he was. He was in such a confused state, he could not tell where he was. With the few vague clues he gave me, I, together with other Christians, tried to find him, but we failed to do so. Two days later, he was found dead at the bottom of Avon Gorge, Bristol. I had to attend the inquest at the Coroner's Court, because I was the last person he spoke to. The coroner brought in an open verdict. Was it merely mental illness that caused him to stumble, or jump off the rocks? If so, who was behind the mental torment? This is just one of the human tragedies that I have encountered, and there are hundreds of them every single day, all over the world.

When we open the newspapers today, we read sickening accounts of how low man has sunk; horrific accounts of rape, murder, cruelty, muggings, child abuse, pain and suffering, rioting, and senseless bombing, where innocent people are killed, or maimed for life, in a so-called just cause. Alcoholism and drug addiction has increased at such a rate the authorities are at a loss as to how to deal with it all. There are just not enough facilities to accommodate the growing numbers of young people who are hooked on drugs, and now we have the added problem of solvent abuse. Incest too, is apparently raising its ugly head in these very troubled times we live in, causing heartbreak and shame to many families.

So is there a devil? The answer must surely be—YES! Behind the terror and evil of our times, there must be a satanic force, stemming from a personal devil. The devil's plan is to distort the truth about himself. He convinces many people that he does not exist, or he will try to give some logical explanation for it all, or contrariwise, he would have some people believe that he has more power than he actually has.

It pleases Satan to strike terror in the human heart, to have men and women cower before him in fear and trembling. Misunderstanding, fear, confusion, disbelief and ignorance, are the handiwork of the devil.

So who exactly is the devil? Where did he come from? What does he really want? How is he working to get it? What is our position as believers? We need to know! When the subject of the devil is clouded with mystery and ignorance, there will be fear and foreboding; but when there is enlightenment and knowledge, the fear is gone.

It is not my intention to glorify the devil in this book, but to make Christians aware of, without being afraid of, the reality of the devil and all his works.

When we explore the tangled scene in the light of God's word, we will find consolation and reassurance that God is still in perfect control of His universe, and His will shall prevail in the end.

If there is anyone who should know whether or not the devil is real, it is me, because I once served him as a satanist and witch, and have first-hand knowledge and experience of his power and how he works. Now I am a Christian, I belong to the Lord Jesus Christ, and have experienced His great power in my life, to save me, and deliver me from the power of the devil, and I know, without a shadow of doubt that God's power is far greater than the devil's power. I can speak plainly, and warn about the devil, without fear. I am not afraid of the devil, and neither should any Christian be. There is no need to fear because God's perfect love casts out all fear, and there is no power, no demon, that can harm me. In God's word we read these wonderful words, ''For I am convinced that neither death nor life, neither angels nor demons, neither the present nor the future, nor any powers, neither height nor depth, nor anything else in all creation, will be able to separate us from the love of God that is in Christ Jesus our Lord'' (Ro 8:38–39). God's shadow is far greater than any fearful shadow of this day and age, and those who abide beneath the shadow of His almighty wings need fear no evil at all.

CHAPTER TWO

God's great mysteries revealed

THE word mystery suggests something obscure, hidden, something strange and unknown. The scriptural use of the word is somewhat different. It refers to some fact or knowledge that God shares with His people. A mystery, in this sense, is that which is not known intellectually, or generally understood, but is revealed by Christ to those who know Him, by the power of the Holy Spirit. This is one of the many benefits enjoyed by the child of God. God does not want us to be in the dark regarding His works or His plans, but He freely shares with us His wisdom and knowledge.

A mystery then, is a previously hidden truth, now revealed by the Spirit of God. God's great mysteries are only revealed to those who accept and believe the Scripture as the Word of God. Christians are able to understand great truths, which the non-believer can never understand or grasp, indeed it is foolishness to them. The apostle Paul says in 1 Corinthians 2:6–8, ''We speak a message of wisdom among the mature, but not the wisdom of this age or of the rulers of this age, who are coming to nothing. No, we speak of God's secret wisdom, a wisdom that has been hidden and that God destined for our glory before time began. None of the rulers of this age understood it, for if they had, they would not have crucified the Lord of glory.'' It goes on to say in verse 10, ''But God has revealed it to us by his Spirit.''

The mysteries of the Kingdom of heaven

Jesus spoke to the multitude in parables: the parable of the sower and his seed; the tares among the wheat; the grain of mustard seed; the leaven in bread; the hidden treasure; the pearl of great price; the fisherman's net. The disciples asked the Lord why He spoke to them in parables, and He answered, that it was because it was given to them to know the mysteries of the Kingdom of heaven, but not to the multitudes, because although they had eyes and ears, they neither saw nor heard, nor understood (Mt 13:11–13). In other words they are blind to the truth. Jesus goes on to say in verse 17, ''Many of the prophets and righteous men longed to see what you see and did not see it, and to hear what you hear but did not hear it.'' Christians are privileged to be able to know and understand, by the Spirit of God, great truths which were hidden even from the prophets in the Old Testament.

Paul says in Romans 16:25–26, ''Now to him who is able to establish you by my gospel and the proclamation of Jesus Christ, according to the revelation of the mystery hidden for long ages past, but now revealed and made known through the prophetic writings by the command of the eternal God, so that all nations might believe and obey him.'' The prophets wrote down what God commanded them to write, although they themselves did not understand the hidden meaning, but it is revealed to those who love and serve the Lord Jesus Christ. Just think about that; it is very wonderful indeed. Everything that God wants us to know about is contained in the Scriptures. It is up to us to search them out and ask God to reveal them to us, and He will.

I have already mentioned one of God's mysteries, the ''mysteries of the Kingdom of heaven'' parables that Jesus taught. There are ten more mysteries, or revealed truths, I would like to point out. They are as follows:

The mystery of the translation of the living saints

Christians refer to this event as ''the rapture'': the time when Jesus will return to this earth to snatch away His waiting people, the body of Christ, His Church, also referred to as "the bride of Christ". These are those who have been washed in the blood of the Lamb, those who have accepted Him as their Lord and Saviour. I believe that Christ is coming back for a radiant church, a purified and victorious church, not a defeated one.

In Matthew 25:1–12 Jesus told the parable of the ten virgins, five of whom were wise, and five foolish. The foolish took their lamps, but they did not take any extra oil with them, but the wise did take extra oil along with their lamps. At midnight the cry went out, "Here's the bridegroom. Come out to meet him." Only the five wise virgins who took the extra oil were ready to meet Him. May we all be prepared, and filled with the oil of the Holy Spirit, when the Lord comes again.

In 1 Corinthians 15:51–52 we read, "Listen, I tell you a mystery: We will not all sleep, but we will all be changed—in a flash, in the twinkling of an eye, at the last trumpet. For the trumpet will sound, the dead will be raised imperishable, and we will be changed." When we speak of the second coming of the Lord to the unbeliever, it's all a mystery to them, they do not understand it at all, but to those who do know the Lord as Saviour, it is a revealed truth and our blessed hope.

The mystery of the body of Christ made up of Jews and Gentiles

Paul speaks in Ephesians 3:2–6 of the mystery made known to him by revelation. He says, "In reading this you will be able to understand my insight into the mystery of Christ, which was not made known to men in other generations as it has now been revealed by the Spirit to God's holy apostles and prophets." Then he goes on to say just what that mystery was, when he says, "This mystery is that through the gospel the Gentiles are heirs together with Israel, members together of one body, and sharers together in the promise in Christ Jesus."

The mystery of the living Christ dwelling in us

Paul was a servant of the Church by God's commission to him to preach the word of God in all its fullness, "the mystery that has been kept hidden for ages and generations, but now is disclosed to the saints" (Col 1:25–27). Then he speaks about the Gentiles again, when he writes in verse 27, "To them God has chosen to make known among the Gentiles the glorious riches of this mystery." He goes on to tell of another mystery, or revealed truth, which is "Christ in you, the hope of glory."

When we know Christ as our Saviour and Lord, He dwells within us. What a wonderful truth! His love reigns in our hearts, His power protects and keeps us, His presence is known to us, and He is precious to us, He is Lord of all.

Does the world at large understand this? To them it is all a great mystery, and many think that Christians are just plain crazy. But to us the living Christ is revealed, and is living in us.

The mystery of the Church as the bride of Christ

After Paul writes about how husbands should love their wives, even as they love themselves, so that the two will become one flesh, he goes on to say, "This is a profound mystery—but I am talking about Christ and the church" (Eph 5:25–32). The unity of husband and wife is compared with Christ and His church; we are members of His body. Christ loved the church and gave Himself up for her, to make her holy, cleansing her by washing with water through the word. Christ wants the church to be radiant, without stain or wrinkle or any other blemish, but holy and blameless. This is indeed a mystery to the unbeliever, but to those who love Christ it is beautiful, it is real.

The mystery of godliness

In 1 Timothy 3, Paul writes of how overseers and deacons should conduct themselves, and says, "If anyone does not know how to manage his own family, how can he take care of God's church?'' He lays down some very good guidelines for them to follow. They must have a good reputation with outsiders, so that they do not fall into disgrace; they must be ''men worthy of respect, sincere, not indulging in much wine, and not pursuing dishonest gain. They must keep hold of the deep truths of the faith with a clear conscience.''

Paul wrote these instructions so they would ''know how to conduct themselves in God's household, which is the church of the living God, the pillar and foundation of the truth.'' Then he says in verse 16, ''Beyond all question, the mystery of godliness is great.'' Man is restored to godliness through the sacrifice of the Lord Jesus Christ. It is His godliness, not our own, and it is very important that Christians conduct themselves in a godly manner both in, and outside, God's house. If outsiders come into God's house and see strife, disorder, confusion and disunity, what kind of testimony is it to them? None at all! It is important then to come into God's house with the right attitudes, displaying all the attributes of godliness. Satan's snare is to rob the children of God of true godliness, giving them a form of godliness, but denying its power (2 Ti 3:5). Some people think that godliness is a means to financial gain, but ''godliness with contentment is great gain'' (1 Ti 6:6). Paul tells us to ''pursue righteousness, godliness, faith, love, endurance and gentleness,'' and ''fight the good fight of faith'' (1 Ti 6:11–12).

Although many non-Christians admire true godliness, they still cannot understand it. Many think that God is a killjoy, and that godly people are miserable people. This again is a clever lie of Satan, because the opposite is true. Real godly people are very happy and contented, for they have the joy of the Lord in their hearts.

The mystery of the Godhead

This mystery reveals that the fullness of the Godhead dwells bodily in the Lord Jesus Christ (Col 2:9). The apostle Paul's purpose was that the saints should be encouraged in heart, and united in love, so they might have complete understanding, in order that they might know "the mysteries of God, namely, Christ, in whom are hidden all the treasures of wisdom and knowledge" (Col 2:2–3).

If Christ is dwelling in us, we too may know His fullness. Christ has all the treasures of wisdom and knowledge. We are *complete* in Him. Christ is head over all other powers and authorities, and as we abide in Him, we too can have power and authority over every opposing force that comes against us, for He has given us His power. We need never be afraid of anything, for God is with us. "We are more than conquerors through Him who loved us." Nothing can "separate us from the love of God that is in Christ Jesus our Lord" (Ro 8:37–38).

The mystery of Israel's blindness to the gospel of Jesus Christ

Paul writes in Romans 11:25, "I do not want you to be ignorant of this mystery, brothers, so that you may not be conceited: Israel has experienced a hardening in part until the full number of the Gentiles has come in. And so all Israel will be saved, as it is written: The deliverer will come from Zion; he will turn godlessness away from Jacob. And this is my covenant with them when I take away their sins."

In the first part of this chapter, Paul tells us that, because of Israel's sin of unbelief, the Gentiles were grafted into the olive tree. Some of the branches have been broken off, and the Gentiles, though a wild olive shoot, have been grafted in among the others, and now share in the nourishing sap from the olive root. If God did not spare the natural branches, the Jews, He will not spare the Gentiles either if they reject Christ. "Branches were broken off so that I could be grafted in" (verse 19). Paul asks, "Did they . . . fall beyond recovery? Not at all! Rather, because of their transgression, salvation has come to the Gentiles" (verse 11). "After all," says Paul in verse 24, "if you were cut out of an olive tree that is wild by nature, and contrary to nature were grafted into a cultivated olive tree, how much more readily will these, the natural branches, be grafted into their own olive tree!'' Many of the Jews have returned, and many are still returning to their homeland, in preparation for the Lord's coming, and many are having their eyes opened to His salvation, through the preaching of the gospel in all nations.

The mystery of the seven stars

In John's revelation on the island of Patmos, he saw seven golden lampstands, and among the lampstands was someone ''like a son of man, dressed in a robe reaching down to his feet and with a golden sash round his chest. His head and hair were white like wool, as white as snow, and his eyes were like blazing fire. His feet were like bronze glowing in a furnace, and his voice was like the sound of rushing waters. In his right hand he held seven stars, and out of his mouth came a sharp double-edged sword. His face was like the sun shining in all its brilliance'' (Rev 1:12–16).

This was a beautiful vision of the living Christ. John was afraid and fell down at His feet, as if dead, but He placed His right hand upon John and said, ''Do not be afraid; I am the First and the Last. I am the living one; I was dead, and behold I am alive for ever and ever.'' He told John to write down all he saw, and all that was about to happen. He told John the meaning of what he saw, and revealed the mystery of the seven stars and the seven lampstands. The seven stars were the angels of the seven churches, and the lampstands were the seven churches (Rev 1:17–20). The angels were not celestial angels, but messengers of God sent to the seven churches with the word of God, which in Scripture is likened to a sharp double-edged sword.

The mystery of Babylon

This mystery will be important to us as we continue to study the mystery of iniquity. The name Babylon is given to a system of apostate religion that is flourishing in our day and age, just as it did in Bible days. It is personified as a prostitute. "This title was written on her forehead: Mystery, Babylon the great, the mother of prostitutes and of the abominations of the earth" (Rev 17:5). John saw this when he was carried away in the Spirit into a desert. He "saw a woman sitting on a scarlet beast that was covered with blasphemous names and had seven heads and ten horns. The woman was dressed in purple and scarlet, and was glittering with gold, precious stones and pearls. She had a golden cup in her hand, filled with abominable things and the filth of her adulteries" (Rev 17:3–4). John was greatly astonished, and the angel said to him, "Why are you astonished? I will explain to you the mystery of the woman and of the beast she rides, which has seven heads and ten horns. The beast, which you saw, once was, now is not, and will come up out of the Abyss and go to his destruction. The inhabitants of the earth whose names have not been written in the book of life from the creation of the world will be astonished when they see the beast, because he once was, now is not, and yet will come" (Rev 17:7–8).

The beast is rearing its head more and more on this earth today, with false prophets bringing false doctrines, false cults and the practice of the occult, with all its abominations. This is Satan's last fling before the end of this age.

Apostate religion is an abandonment of true religion for the false. James says, "Religion that God our father accepts as pure and faultless is this: to look after orphans and widows in their distress and to keep oneself from being polluted by the world" (Jas 1:27).

The apostate religious system in these dark days, whatever form it takes, will be filled with such sin and iniquity that God Himself will bring the final judgment upon it. "For her sins are piled up to heaven, and God has remembered her crimes" (Rev 18:5).

I like what it says in Revelation 17:14, "They will

make war against the Lamb, but the Lamb will overcome them because he is Lord of lords and King of
kings—and with him will be his called, chosen and
faithful followers.''

The mystery of iniquity

In 2 Thessalonians 2:7 we read, ''For the mystery of
iniquity doth already work'' (AV). If God by His Holy
Spirit can reveal the mysteries I have named, why not
the mystery of iniquity? He does not want us to be
ignorant about the times we are living in, where Satan is
working overtime in a futile effort to overthrow Christianity, where there is chaos, disorder and fear. Paul
said it was already at work in his day, but is increasing
in our day, and it will increase and intensify as the days
get shorter and Christ's return nears. This will be a
revelation of truth, which can be traced in the Scriptures right from the very beginning up to this present
day and age. We need a fresh revelation today of God's
word. God's people are far too gullible, and sad to say,
it is our own fault. Are we truly examining everything
in the light of God's word? Are we truly examining
those who come into our midst, saying they have been
sent by the Lord? We should not be tossed about with
every wind of doctrine, for there are so many false
prophets today.

We must become more mature in our ability to discern
between that which is of Christ and that which is not.
Any teaching that is presented which is contrary to the
written word of God must be rejected by the church of
Jesus Christ. The Scriptures are not to be added to, or
subtracted from. The right hand of Christ, which John
saw holding the seven stars, represents Christ's absolute power and authority. When the word of Christ
comes forth from the mouth of Christ, through His servants who are God's appointed ministers, it is more
powerful than any other weapon in the whole universe.
''The word of God is living and active. Sharper than
any double-edged sword, it penetrates even to dividing

soul and spirit, joints and marrow; it judges the thoughts and attitudes of the heart. Nothing in all creation is hidden from God's sight. Everything is uncovered and laid bare before the eyes of him to whom we must give account'' (Heb 4:12–13). John saw Christ standing among the lampstands, which are the churches. Christ still stands in the midst of His church, and His eyes of fire search every single motive and deed. His voice was like the sound of many waters, and the voice of Jesus Christ is absolute power, absolute authority, absolute wisdom. That voice is multiplied today in the body of Christ's church, the people out of whom flow ''rivers of living water.''

If believers are to grow to maturity, they must also share in the ministries of the church. We cannot mature on our own, or be conquerors in Christ on our own. We need each other's fellowship and prayers. We need regular instruction and teaching from God's word in order for us to grow, and receive revelation from God's word. Believers must be willing to obey the leadership which God places in the church, men who are to be mature and steadfast, and filled with the Holy Spirit, fully yielded to Christ, keeping hold of the truths of God's word. Believers should take part in the corporate life-flow of Christ's church. There are too many who are doing their own thing, going their own way. It is dangerous to go your own way—you can fall into deception, which leads away from God's word. The revelation of the mystery of iniquity is not my own, it is not coming from my own mind; it has been revealed through careful reading and study of God's word. It is important to note that God will only reveal to us what he wants us to know about iniquity, because God does not want us to dwell upon dark and evil things to the extent that we lose all blessing and peace. God shows us in the Bible how Satan deceived our first parents, and how he worked against mankind in the beginning, and shows us how to overcome him today. The mystery of iniquity will be explained further in the following chapters, which cover a range of subjects.

John saw seven stars, and seven lampstands. Seven is the number of perfection, completeness, and wholeness. Christ is perfecting His church today, opening its eyes to deep hidden truths in His word, filling His people with His wisdom and knowledge. The mystery of iniquity need not remain a total mystery. There are some things we do not understand, let us not forget that God only wants the very best for the creation He has made, and will only show us what He wants us to know to make us aware of the devil's tactics, thus equipping us to conquer the foe, through Christ's power in our lives.

The origin and fall of Satan

TO many, the origin of sin and its continued exist-ence, is a source of mystery, perplexity and confusion. They see the works of evil all around them, and its terrible results, and question how all this can exist under an eternal God of love. In their uncertainty and doubt they eventually come to believe that God does not exist. The belief in evolution is very widespread, but those who believe in the gradual development of the species from earlier forms of life will not find the answers to their questions, and can never be clear-cut about the power and presence of evil.

True Christians however, believe what the Bible says; "In the beginning God created the heavens and the earth" (Ge 1:1). Note, God created the heavens *before* He created the earth. In John 1:1 we read, "In the beginning was the Word, and the Word was with God, and the Word was God." Christ the Word was with God in the beginning, all things were created by Him. Christ, the only begotten of God, was one with the Father: one in nature, character and purpose, and the only one who could enter into all the counsel and purposes of God. Through Christ the eternal Father brought into being all the angels, cherubim, and seraphim. "For by him all things were created: things in heaven and on earth, visible and invisible, whether thrones or powers or rulers or authorities; all things were created by him and for him" (Col 1:16). Lucifer, now called Satan or the devil, was created as a beautiful guardian cherub.

Ezekiel 28:2–19 and Isaiah 14:12–17 give us a clear picture of Lucifer before sin entered his heart and he became Satan. Let us look at how he was created.

He was created by God alone and therefore dependant upon God for his existence. He was perfect when he was created (Eze 28:15) and perfect in his beauty, and full of wisdom (Eze 28:12). He was in Eden, the garden of God, and was decked with many precious stones, set in pure gold (Eze 28:13). He was a guardian cherub, placed by God to cover the throne of God (Eze 28:14–16). Compare this with the cherubim who covered the mercy seat, on the ark of the covenant in the tabernacle of Moses (Ex 37:9). He was also an anointed being, just as the Old Testament priests, prophets and kings. He was called "morning star, son of the dawn" (Isa 14:12). He was on the holy mountain of God (Eze 28:14). How very beautiful he must have been! He was made with music in his being, "The workmanship of thy tabrets and of thy pipes was prepared in thee in the day that thou wast created" (Eze 28:13 AV). He could have been the leader of the heavenly choirs.

It is important to note that Lucifer was created this way by God himself. He does not exist by or of himself. Neither did God create him as a mere force of evil but a very real heavenly being. There is a human tendency to think that the devil is just a force of evil, rather like a very strong wind. There is also a tendency to believe that two great powers exist, one good, the other evil, and the two are equal. Whilst it is true that two powers do exist; one good, the other evil, one from God, the other from Satan, it is by no means true that the two are equal. God is the creator, therefore His power is far greater.

Lucifer once held a very high position in heaven and had angels directly under his authority, who delighted to do his bidding. All heaven was his, all the heavenly beings reflected the glory of their creator, and worshipped God in adoration and praise. We read in the Bible, "The morning stars sang together and all the

34

angels shouted for joy'' (Job 38:7). Sin then entered into the heart of Lucifer, we are not told how. There are many people today who get really confused about this; they cannot understand how sin entered the heart of this cherub, and why God allowed sin in heaven at all. If God wanted us to know this, He would have told us, but He did not tell us; all we are told is what is written in the Scriptures, and that is all we need to know. A note of discord must have marred the celestial harmonies when sin entered into the heart of Lucifer. Lucifer became full of pride because of his brightness and wisdom, and he said in his heart ''I will be like the most high.''

He became jealous of God's glory, and was discontented with his high office. He was ungrateful for the honours conferred upon him, and he aspired to be equal with God, his creator. It is noteworthy that it was in the heart that sin was first conceived. Isaiah 14:12–15 gives us details of Lucifer's iniquity and his fivefold plan of rebellion. Let us examine this fivefold plan of Satan's, taking our headings from the authorised version of the scriptures.

I will ascend into heaven

What does this mean, as Satan was already in heaven? Lucifer dared to aspire to a domain reserved for deity. There are levels, or stages in heaven as the apostle Paul intimated in his testimony that either in a vision or in his body, he had been caught up to the third heaven. It is accepted that the earth's atmosphere is the first heaven, the starry universe the second, and the abode of God the third. From an analysis of the further goals that Satan stated, we know that his ambition was to be like God. He who had been created by God now aspired to be like God and usurp His authority. He who had been created full of wisdom had now, by his iniquity, become filled with evil folly. He was jealous of all God had that he did not have, and conspired to enter into God's holy place, a place reserved for the Godhead alone.

I will exalt my throne above the stars of God

Lucifer's ambition included lordship and rulership over God's creation. At this point in Satan's rebellious plan there is an explicit reference to divine sovereignty and rulership from the very throne from which God rules creation. The hosts of heaven are sometimes referred to as the stars of God (Job 38:7). The word *star* is frequently used as a figurative reference to Christ and His church (Nu 24:17, Rev 1:16–20), also in Revelation 22:16 where we read ''I, Jesus, have sent my angel to give you this testimony for the churches. I am the Root and the Offspring of David, and the bright Morning *Star*.'' The intention of Lucifer was to assert supremacy over all the celestial creation of God, by being like his creator in every way, including having his own throne.

I will sit also upon the mount of the congregation, in the sides of the north

Satan's ambition was to rule the universe, and gain its worship. This scheme of Satan's, emphasises his intention to control the world's religion. The word *mount* suggests rulership, and the word *congregation* suggests worship (see Isa 2:2 AV). In Psalm 48:2 we read, ''Beautiful for situation, the joy of the whole earth, is mount Zion, on the sides of the north, the city of the great King.'' This psalm refers to Jerusalem, the spiritual centre of Jewish and Christian faith, and it is spoken of in a language similar to that Satan used. Now Lucifer's plan is made more clear. He would rule the universe, and all creation would worship him as well as God his creator, in the city of God, in Mount Zion on the sides of the north, the city of the great King.

I will ascend above the heights of the clouds

Clouds have always been associated in the Scripture with the glory of God. During the wilderness journeys of the Israelites, it was an accompanying cloud that represented the guiding presence of God, "Behold the glory of the Lord appeared in the cloud" (Ex 16:10 AV). God manifested Himself in clouds during the wilderness journeys, as when the tabernacle was completed, "Then the cloud covered the Tent of Meeting, and the glory of the Lord filled the tabernacle" (Ex 40:34). When Solomon completed his great temple of the Lord, "the cloud filled the temple of the Lord. And the priests could not perform their service because of the cloud, for the glory of the Lord filled his temple" (1 Ki 8:10–11).

Lucifer wanted to be equal with God and share God's glory, thus deflecting the glory from God alone. He wanted to sit where God sits. Whenever we see "glory" mentioned it speaks of the dwelling place of the Godhead, a place for God alone. What rebellion! What jealousy! At the second coming of Christ, He will be revealed, "on the clouds of the sky, with power and great glory" (Mt 24:30). Lucifer desired no other glory but his own, no other power or authority above his own. Such arrogance staggers the mind. It was insane, because there was no possibility of success, but he pursued it nevertheless, and he still pursues it today.

I will be like the most High

At last, Lucifer makes his evil plan complete by placing himself in direct comparison with God. He has mentioned heaven, the stars of God, His Holy Mount, the clouds of His glory, and now lastly he states his intention towards God Himself. He would be like Him. He, who had the highest place in God's creation now aspired to be higher still. He, who was the wisest and the most beautiful, now desired to be all-wise. He wanted to be omniscient: to know all things. He was powerful, but he wanted to be all-powerful. He wanted to be omnipotent. He was able to go anywhere his creator willed him to go, but he wanted to be everywhere. He wanted to be omnipresent. What rebellion! What deception!

He did not hold to the truth, he became a liar and a murderer. He was self-deceived (Jn 8:44). He was the original sinner; iniquity was first found in him (Eze 28:15–16). He is the original antichrist (2 Th 2:7 and Ge 3:1–6). He is a thief (Jn 10:10). He is a fowler, who traps and ensnares (Ps 91:3). He masquerades as an angel of light (2 Co 11:14). He is the source of all sin, and in him the mystery of iniquity is personified. Because of his iniquity Satan was cast out of heaven, and Jesus saw him fall, for we read in Luke 10:18, "I saw Satan fall like lightning from heaven."

Satan did not fall alone

Lucifer influenced a large part of the heavenly host. We get some idea of his authority from Revelation 12:9, "The great dragon was hurled down, that ancient serpent called the devil, or Satan, who leads the whole world astray. He was hurled to the earth, and his angels with him." It is very revealing to read that the angels who fell with him are referred to as *his* angels. It shows you what power and authority he once had in heaven. No, Satan did not fall alone, and it is my belief that he was not cast out immediately sin was conceived in his heart. I am convinced that he had to work over a period of time, in order to influence the angels under him.

I believe he worked with great and mysterious secrecy, and concealed his real purpose under a pretence of reverence to God, although it is certain that God was not fooled by this. He was greatly loved and respected by the heavenly hosts; and as someone as high as he was, an anointed cherub, he was highly exalted, and his influence was very strong. I believe he sought to create sympathy for himself, and his cause, by stirring up discontent among the other angels, and trying to influence them, as well as those who were directly under him.

I can imagine this lofty cherub questioning ''Why should Christ have the supremacy? Why is Christ honoured above me?'' The angels had no knowledge of sin, they could not discern the consequences that would result from this rebellion. I believe that Satan lied to the angels under him, telling them that they too could gain a higher place in the heavenly sphere if they followed him. We are told in the Bible, ''And there was war in heaven. Michael and his angels fought against the dragon, and the dragon and his angels fought back. But he was not strong enough, and they lost their place in heaven'' (Rev 12:7-8).

It is difficult to imagine a war in heaven, but that is what the Bible says happened. The angels were deceived by Satan, whose power to deceive is very great, and I believe he disguised himself in a cloak of falsehood and gained an advantage and his high position gave greater force to his lies, and many were induced to rebel with him. Rebellion is a grave sin against God, and in God's word we are told that it is like the sin of witchcraft.

We read in Revelation 12:4 that a third of the host of heaven rebelled, and fell with Satan. That might seem like a lot of angels, but there are billions and billions left, which make up a far greater army than that of the devil; so there is no need to fear.

God's angels protect the children of God. There are instances recorded in the Bible where angels protected and aided God's servants. We have a guardian angel who watches over us, and protects us, if we obey the Lord and walk in His ways.

Satan's plans for supremacy came to nothing, because Michael and his angels fought against him, and Satan and his angels were cast out of heaven (Rev 12:7-9). Now united with Satan, they have through all succeeding ages co-operated with him in his warfare against divine authority. We are told in the Scriptures of their confederacy and subtlety, and their malicious designs against the peace and happiness of man.

Under Satan's control there are a vast number of demons, who obey his every command. They make up a very strong, and highly organised army, and represent him and his evil cause all over the world. But the very fact that Satan has to rely on them to do much of his work, proves how limited he is. Because although he lusted for omnipresence, he did not get it. The demons who represent him, however, are capable of travelling in a split second to any given place at any given time.

Only God our creator is omnipresent. Even I, when I was a Satanist, knew that Satan was not omnipresent. When he appeared in one of the temples of Satan (and he did appear), we all knew it was Satan, and not one of his demon spirits. We knew that while Satan was there, he was nowhere else in the whole universe.

Many Christians do not realise this truth, they seem to think that the devil is everywhere at the same time. I wish Christians would grasp the truth that the devil is not omnipresent, and therefore limited in where he can go.

The vast army of demon spirits under Satan's control are referred to in various ways in the Bible. They are called deceiving spirits, principalities, powers, rulers of darkness, wicked spirits and demons. These different titles suggest different stages, or levels of authority in Satan's kingdom. Although many believe that these names refer to the same beings, there is a difference. For instance, deceiving spirits deceive the world in many ways, and wicked spirits incite great wickedness, and so on; and there is a difference between demons and fallen angels. This is another study, so I am just touching briefly on this subject. It has been made clear that when Satan fell, a third of the heavenly host fell with him, preferring to do his bidding than God's.

There are two scriptures however, that have caused confusion to some Christians; namely 2 Peter 2:4, ''For if God did not spare angels when they sinned, but sent them to hell, putting them into gloomy dungeons to be held for judgment'' . . . And Jude 6, ''And the angels who did not keep their positions of authority but abandoned their own home—these he has kept in darkness, bound with everlasting chains for judgment on the great Day.'' So how, Christians ask, can demons be responsible for evil on the earth, if they have been bound in chains, and cast down to hell to await judgment?

Here I would like to expose the teaching of modern-day satanism, which should throw some light on the subject. As a one-time satanist and witch, I can tell you that the following facts are true. This teaching was first presented to the ancient priests, when Satan himself appeared in the first satanist temple many thousands of years ago; at least this is what I was taught, and what is written in the satanist bible, and other ancient manuscripts.

Satanists do not teach that God does not exist, and Satan exists alone. On the contrary, they teach that God does indeed exist, but they teach that Satan is also a God in his own right. What is more they teach that Satan had a part in creating the heaven and the earth. It is important for Christians to know the teaching of the satanists, because it will open their eyes to the audacity of Satan. Satan is saying he is a god, and always was a god, he is saying he and our true God were dual gods working together, and they made the world together; that Lucifer was not created, but was like God. This is what Satan lusted for, but did not get, so he then started teaching people on the earth that he was equal with God, teaching that Jehovah God was unjust to Lucifer, and did not give to Lucifer equal power and authority in heaven.

Moreover, they teach that because of God's unjust treatment, Satan's rebellion was justified. When Satan stood up for his rights for equal power, God ordered the Archangel Michael and his angels, who were stronger than Satan's angels, to overpower Satan's strongest angels, and bind them in chains and cast Satan and the rest of his angels out of heaven. Furthermore, they go on to teach that one day Satan will gain strength to regain his place in heaven, by recruiting people on this earth who will be, in fact, "the devil's angels" who will assist his angels, and he will rescue the angels that God bound in chains, overthrow the hosts of heaven (including God himself), and Satan will then rule the whole universe. Satan creates sympathy for himself from his followers with this false and evil teaching. So, the more people who follow Satan and do his will on this earth, the more wickedness that is done, the sooner Satan will rule, they say. Satan is a liar and the father of lies, and this lie really shows how he goes on from one lie to another, thus confirming that he is indeed the father of lies.

You may wonder why Satan reveals that more wickedness must be done, in order to do what he says he will do; surely this in itself gives the game away; surely this reveals that he is evil and people will not want to serve him. Satan always oversteps his mark, and shows himself as he really is, but still people are willing to be deluded by him. Satan has to go along with all his teachings, which also contradict each other. One of the teachings of the satanists is that evil is good and good is evil, darkness is light and light is darkness. When we read Isaiah 5:20 we see clearly that people did this then, and are still doing it today. Everything the devil does is twisted, just as he himself is twisted. All the teachings of Satan are false, and a perversion of the truth. Satan does not deal with whole lies, they would be too easily discerned. He takes half-truths, and turns them into lies. It is far easier to deceive when the truth is mixed with lies, and made to appear wholly true. It is important that Christians know how he twists things; this makes Satan the greatest twister of all time.

It also reveals to us how desperate Satan is, because he knows his end is drawing near. He oversteps his mark by revealing how limited he is without the angels of God bound in chains, who rebelled with him. We should at least rejoice to know how limited he is. What God has bound is bound, Satan cannot loose anything. All evil spirits that are now working on this earth will be joining those whom God has bound in chains, and they will all be cast into the lake of fire.

Satan is always ready to supply the desires of the human heart, and palms off his deception in the place of the truth, and he spreads his net where least expected. If people would only read and study the word of truth with earnest prayer, that they would understand the deep truths of God's word, they would not be left in any doubt regarding it, and less open to receiving false doctrine. Some people do not want to receive the truth, and the apostle Paul speaks about those who refuse to love the truth, that they may be saved. He declares, ''For this reason God sends them a powerful delusion so that they will believe the lie and so that all will be condemned who have not believed the truth but have delighted in wickedness.'' (2 Th 2:11–12).

Later on in this book I will reveal further evil teachings and works of Satan, and open people's eyes to his subtlety. When Jesus walked this earth, He cast out many demons that possessed people, and set those people free from Satan's power. If every single angel that rebelled with Satan, and was cast out of heaven, were bound in chains, they could not possess, oppress, depress or distress anyone, and there would have been no demons for Jesus to cast out. So it is plain to me that only a certain number of the angels who rebelled with Satan were bound in chains, and the rest assist Satan today in his work upon the earth. But it is very important to remember that Satan cannot do all the evil on his own, and has to rely on the demons to do it, and this should be an encouragement to every Christian. God has many more angels, who do the perfect will of God, and make up a far greater and more powerful army than that of the devil, and these angels are on our side.

When Satan lost his place in heaven, he also lost his heavenly body and his heavenly name, Lucifer. In the satanist movement, however, he is always referred to as Lucifer, not the devil, or Satan, or any other name, just Lucifer. He still wants to be known by his original name. That does not alter the fact that he lost all he had before he fell from heaven. He is now known in the Scriptures by many names. In Scripture the name of a person usually depicts the nature, experience, or function of the person named. This is true of the many names of God. This is also true of Satan. His name shows who he is, and how he works. Here are some names by which Satan is known, or recognised, today:

Satan: Adversary, Hater, Opponent, Enemy—1 Pe 5:8, Job 1:6–12, 2:1–7.
Serpent: Enchanter, Beguiler—Ge 3:1–14, Rev 12:9, 20:2.
Prince of this world: Jn 12:31, 14:30, 16:11.
Man of lawlessness: 2 Th 2:3–4.
Ruler of the kingdom of the air: Eph 2:2.
Fowler: One who traps and ensnares—Ps 91:3.
Accuser of the brethren: Rev 12:10.
Angel of light: 2 Co 11:13–15.
Wolf, **Thief**, **Robber**: Jn 10:10.

So now we see Satan has lost his place in heaven, his heavenly body, and his name. But did he then give up? No! He still plots and plans. He did not give up his plans, he simply revised his strategy, but not his aims, as we shall see as we continue to trace the pattern of apostasy and rebellion.

CHAPTER FOUR

The origin and fall of man

ALMOST every known villain recorded in history did not set out to become a villain; they were first of all filled with evil pride, just as Satan was in the beginning. Satan did not intend to fall, or lose his place, but to rise up, and gain a much higher one.

One such villain readily springs to mind—Adolf Hitler. He did not intend to become a monster, to be loathed; he had far more splendid ideas than that. He viewed himself as a great champion, a powerful leader, one to be admired and adored. He was self-deceived, believing that the master race, as he called it, would rule the world, and he would be their leader. He would stop at nothing to achieve this, going as far as trying to wipe out the Jewish race completely.

The Jews have always been known as God's chosen people. Hitler was an atheist, so the Jews posed a threat to him and his evil plans, so he told his leaders that the Jews were an inferior race, and he intended to get rid of them. The fact was, they were a very superior people, a powerful people, and there were too many of them for Hitler's comfort. His twisted mind was so perverted, he saw his cause to be proper and good. Those like him, before and after him, who lusted for power, yet brought about horror, destruction and death, were inspired by nothing else but demon power. It all goes back to the beginning, in the garden of Eden.

When God made man, which was after Satan was ejected from heaven, Satan was intensely jealous, just as he was when he was in heaven. Satan was created,

God created him, and Satan himself could not create anything so he was jealous of God's creative powers. Now God had made Adam and Eve, and God created them with some of His own attributes. Man and woman were made in the image of God, and everything that God made was good (Ge 1:31). Satan's envy was so fierce, so strong, as he gazed at the beautiful couple, the beautiful home God had made for them, and the sweet fellowship God had with them, that he was determined to cause their fall. Not satisfied with bringing about the fall of some of the angels, he now sought the downfall of human beings. Satan turned his attention towards man, and he has been doing so ever since.

Satan employed for his medium the serpent, who was then a creature of fascination and beautiful appearance. The serpent in his Edenic form is not to be thought of as a writhing reptile; that was the effect of the curse. The serpent that lent himself to Satan may well have been the most beautiful of creatures. Traces of that beauty still remain despite the curse. Every movement of the serpent is graceful, and many species are beautifully coloured. Had Satan appeared in his own form, which was ugly and dark, Adam and Eve may well have been repelled at once, so he took on a form that was beautiful, concealing his real purpose so that he might more effectually accomplish his aim. He still does the same thing today. He makes sin appear lovely, inviting, and even good, to attract us and cause us to sin.

The very first thing the serpent said to Eve was, "Did God really say, 'You must not eat from any tree in the garden'?" (Ge 3:1), sowing a seed of doubt in the mind of Eve as to what God had really said. Had Eve refused to enter into conversation with the serpent, she would have been safe, but she chose to parley with him, and fell a victim to his wiles. God made Adam and Eve with a free will; Eve did not have to listen to the serpent, she could have walked away.

It is the same today. People choose to doubt and argue about the commandments of God; instead of accepting His divine commands, they accept human theories, which are just a disguise of Satan's wiles.

"The woman said to the serpent, 'We may eat fruit from the trees in the garden, but God did say, "You must not eat fruit from the tree that is in the middle of the garden, and you must not touch it, or you will die"'" (Ge 3:2–3). "'You will not surely die,'" said the serpent (suggesting God was untruthful), "'your eyes will be opened, and you will be like God, knowing good and evil.'" Being like God, remember, is what Satan himself desired before he fell. Eve was deceived by the serpent, and yielded to temptation, and through her influence, Adam was also led into sin.

Satan lead Adam and Eve to distrust their creator, and to believe God had restricted them by withholding wisdom and knowledge from them. It is the same today. Satan suggests to mankind that God restricts people, taking away their freedom and liberty, and that Christianity is oppressive and cruel. Adam and Eve's disobedience was a great triumph for Satan, for with it sin passed into the human race (Ro 5:12).

Their sin had separated them from God, so they could no longer enjoy direct fellowship with God. It would now mean that man would need a mediator to reconcile him to God. The first promise of a Redeemer is given in Genesis 3:15, "'And I will put enmity between you and the woman, and between your offspring and hers; he will crush your head, and you will strike his heel.'"

We read in Isaiah 53:5, "But he was pierced for our transgressions, He was crushed for our iniquities." When Satan heard God's curse on him, he must have trembled, for he knew that his efforts to deprave the human race would one day be interrupted by means of a Saviour, who would reconcile man to God.

The enemy of Christ and His followers is Satan, and the enemy of Satan is Christ and His followers. Jesus once said to those who were against Him, "You belong to your father, the devil, and you want to carry out your father's desire" (Jn 8:44).

Jesus also called the devil a liar, and the father of lies.

It is only the grace of Christ implanted in our hearts which creates in us enmity against Satan. Satan's enmity against the human race is kindled by the knowledge that believers are, through Christ's death on Calvary, objects of God's mercy and grace.

The words of Satan to Eve, 'Your eyes will be opened' proved true only in this sense, their eyes were opened to discern their folly; they knew evil, and they tasted the bitter fruit of transgression. Until fully developed, sin does not appear the evil thing it really is.

Let us look at the consequences of Adam and Eve's sin, a condition which must remain until the Kingdom age, when Christ rules the earth.

1. The serpent, Satan's tool is cursed (Ge 3:14, Ro 16:20) and becomes God's graphic warning in nature of the effects of sin—the most beautiful and subtle of creatures becomes a loathsome reptile. The deepest mystery of the cross of Christ is strikingly pictured by a serpent of bronze, a type of Christ made sin for us; bearing punishment we deserved (Nu 21:6–9, Jn 3:14–15, 2 Co 5:21).
2. The light occupation of Eden is changed to burdensome labour (Ge 3:17–19).
3. The woman's state is changed, in respect of her increased pain in childbirth, and in the headship of the man (Ge 3:16). Sin's disorder makes necessary a headship, which is vested in man (Eph 5:23, 1 Ti 2:11–14).
4. The brevity of life and the tragic certainty of physical death to Adam and his descendants (Ge 3:19).

In the middle of the garden grew the tree of life whose fruit had the power of perpetuating life. Had Adam and Eve remained obedient to God, they would have had continued access to this tree, and lived forever. By partaking of the tree of knowledge of good and evil, they became subject to death. God banished them from the garden and placed the cherubim, and a flaming sword to guard the way to the tree of life. God had to banish them from the garden, or they would have eaten from the tree of life in their sinful state, thus condemning man to everlasting life with a sinful nature.

The wages of sin is death, both physical and spiritual; the gift of eternal life can only come from Christ, who shed His blood at Calvary that we might live.

From the days of Adam to our own time, our great enemy, the devil, has been exercising his power to destroy and oppress. All who know Christ will in one way or another be brought into conflict with this relentless foe. All who actively engage in the cause against Satan and sin, seeking to expose his deceptions and present Christ to the world, will be the target of Satan, but Christ will give power and strength to overcome him day by day. No-one can be overcome unwillingly, the tempter has no power to control the will or force the soul to sin. The very fact that Christ conquered death at Calvary should inspire His followers to fight the good fight of faith, with courage in their hearts. Satan may distress us, but he can't contaminate; he can cause agony, but not defilement. Let us think of that lovely scripture in Romans 8:35–37, ''Who shall separate us from the love of Christ? Shall trouble or hardship or persecution or famine or nakedness or danger or sword? As it is written: 'For your sake we face death all day long; we are considered as sheep to be slaughtered.' No, in all these things we are more than conquerors through Him who loved us.'' In the following chapter we will be looking at how Satan worked until Christ came into the world, to make a way back to God for mankind.

CHAPTER FIVE

A religious devil

SATAN is consistently, emphatically religious. Religious but not Christian, and not holy. Although he declared his intention to attain God's throne, he nowhere mentioned any desire for the holiness of God.

As long as people enjoyed creator fellowship with God, there was no place for the devil. It was therefore essential for Satan to drive a greater wedge between God and man. We have seen his vile footsteps in the garden of Eden, in his first encounter with Adam and Eve and his success in disrupting the simple fellowship and communion they had with God. This disruption became even more pronounced as time passed, for even after the great flood God sent upon the earth because of man's wickedness, people continued to break God's laws.

Satan is basically religious, and wants to be worshipped. Under his deceitful influences, the inherent need to worship was perverted, leading people to worship false gods. In fact, their devotion was turned to the devil, who hid behind many guises and names. People forgot God and became entangled in perverted and horrible practices of worship. Except for the true faith of God held by the children of Abraham, the world became filled with apostasy.

We read in the Scriptures "Certain men, the children of Belial, are gone out from among you, and have withdrawn the inhabitants of their city, saying, 'Let us go and serve other gods, which ye have not known.'" (Dt 13:13 AV).

In the Old Testament, Satan was frequently referred to as Belial, a profane and worthless one. The devil does not discourage worship, he perverts it with lies and deception, and turns it towards himself.

People came to worship many things under the deception of Satan; the sun, the moon, the stars, fire, water, and almost every natural feature of the earth. To these were added earth's creatures, such as the bull, the monkey, the cat, the cow, the jackal, the wolf, the eagle, and above all—the serpent. We read in Romans 1:21–25 exact details of how, and what, people worshipped. "Although they claimed to be wise, they became fools and exchanged the glory of the immortal God for images made to look like mortal man and birds and animals and reptiles. . . . They exchanged the truth of God for a lie, and worshipped and served created things rather than the Creator" (Ro 1:22–23, 25). People still do the same thing today. Some really believe that the planetary system affects their lives. Some worship the moon, others the stars, some the power of fire. Although it all sounds stupid, it is a fact.

Among the deities mentioned in the Scriptures are the human leaders of the nations: the pharaohs of Egypt, the kings of Babylon, Assyria and others. In addition to these deities which could be seen with human eyes, people, through the influence of Satan, invented a multitude of invisible gods.

Egypt had literally hundreds of gods: Horus, Osiris, Amon, Ptah, and many more. In the midst of all the religious confusion was Israel, where the worship of Jehovah was preserved, which made the Israelites a very special people. Yet the devil repeatedly, and persistently, introduced other forms of worship into the land, to contaminate the pure worship of God.

Although the Israelites were led out of slavery in the land of Egypt, by the divine hand of God, they still inclined to worship the gods of Egypt. The people demanded of Aaron, "Come, make us gods who will go before us. As for this fellow Moses who brought us up

51

out of Egypt, we don't know what has happened to him.'' (Ex 32:1).

The bull god Apis, sacred to the Egyptians, was the model of a calf of gold which the newly freed Hebrew slaves worshipped. They decided they wanted to worship, and worship they did.

They wanted an object they could see and touch, something to excite the imagination. Satan took advantage of their confused emotions, and reminded them of their past life in Egypt, and the gods of Egypt. They demanded that Aaron make a golden calf for them and gladly gave up their gold for its construction.

The bull god Apis represented a sexual imagery, in its association with the procreative energies of the bull, which inspires sensual worship. Under the influence of Satan its worshippers could experience awe, excitement and release in an orgy of worship.

This bull god, Apis, which modern-day satanists call a demon god, is still worshipped in satanist temples and black witches' covens. When I first became a Christian and started to read my Bible, I was so surprised to find that many of the gods worshipped and called upon by satanists were mentioned in both the Old and New Testaments. I could hardly believe it at first, but it helped me to understand spiritual warfare, and opened my eyes to the reality of deception. It proved to me how very methodical Satan is, and proved beyond a shadow of a doubt that devil worship is as ancient as the world itself.

In the end, it was Israel's worship of the gods of Canaan that caused their exile from their homeland. We read in 2 Kings 17 just how wicked they had become. They just did not take heed of the warnings, so the Lord rejected them and gave them into the hands of the plunderers (verse 20). We read a long list of their evil acts in this chapter. I will quote a few of them:

''[They] secretly did things against the Lord their God that were not right. From watchtower to fortified city

they built themselves high places in all their towns"
(verse 9).

"They set up sacred stones and Asherah poles on
every high hill and under every spreading tree"
(verse 10).

"At every high place they burned incense" (verse
11).

"They worshipped idols, though the Lord had
said, 'You shall not do this'" (verse 12).

"They followed worthless idols and themselves
became worthless" (verse 15).

"They forsook all the commands of the Lord their
God and made for themselves two idols cast in the
shape of calves" (verse 16).

"They sacrificed their sons and daughters in the
fire. They practised divination and sorcery and sold
themselves to do evil in the eyes of the Lord, pro-
voking Him to anger" (verse 17).

This is what the Lord said would happen, and it happened: "The Lord will scatter you among the peoples,
and only a few of you will survive among the nations to
which the Lord will drive you. There you will worship
man-made gods of wood and stone, which cannot see
or hear or eat or smell" (Dt 4:27–28).

Let us take a closer look at these gods. Baal (plural
Baalim) was a god of the Canaanites. The Baalim were
worshipped in nature, outdoors on high hills in forest
groves (Dt 12:2–3, Jdg 6:25, 1 Ki 16:31–33). The worship
of Baal was deep-rooted in the land and proved a lasting
confusion to Israel.

Although various godly men tried to stamp it out, the
worship of Baal lasted for years. What most people do
not know is that Baal is still called upon in many black
witches' covens today. Mother earth is regarded as a
great goddess—forests and hills are still the favourite
place for witches, and Baal is still worshipped today.
The Baal (sun or lord) was the supreme divinity of the
Phoenician and Canaanite nations. Ashtoreth was their
supreme female divinity. We find her worship well

established among the Moabites, and their allies the Midianites, in the time of Moses. Through these nations the Israelites were seduced to worship this god, under the form of Baal Peor (Nu 25:3).

The worship of Baal among the Jews appeared to be appointed with much pomp and ceremony, for temples were erected to him (2 Ki 11:18). The worshippers appear to have been arrayed in appropriate robes (2 Ki 10:22) and worshipped by burning incense (Jer 11:13). The worship of Baal in the satanist temples today is almost identical, with pomp and ceremony, robes and incense. Satan worship is not new, it was with us before the flood.

The goddess Ashtoreth was worshipped widely along the coasts of Palestine. She was a goddess of fertility, and was worshipped with lewd sexual rites. The Hebrews forsook the Lord and served Baal and Ashtoreth (Jdg 2:12–13). They were both worshipped with licentious sexual acts in groves and high places.

During the lifetime of Samuel he influenced the people to return to God and abandon the worship of Baal and Ashtoreth (1 Sa 7:3–4). Ashtoreth is still worshipped today and held in great esteem among witches, black and white. The very same things go on today in covens as in Old Testament times.

Dagon was the chief deity of the Philistines. Although the Jews did not widely serve him, his cult was well established, and a huge temple was erected for it. It was in this temple of Dagon that Saul's head was displayed after his defeat by the Philistines. When the ark of God was captured it was put in Dagon's vile temple, but the image collapsed in the presence of the ark, which represented the true God. Even when they put his images back, the next morning, its hands and its head were broken off, and only his body remained (1 Sa 5:1–6). It was the temple of Dagon that Samson destroyed (Jdg 16:23–30).

When Satan introduced the vile god Molech, it plainly showed the basest side of his evil nature. Molech was worshipped by means of human sacrifice, especially the sacrifice of children.

54

The Jews allegiance to God had really sunk low, when they were willing to sacrifice their own children to this false and cruel god. Before they entered Canaan God had warned them against this terrible practice (Lev 20:2–5). The warning went unheeded. They still went ahead and did things which can only be described as barbarous. Huge images of Molech (Malcam or Milcam as the god was variously called), were erected in Israel. His arms were used as fiery altars, where children were burned in sacrifice to satisfy the hunger of this cruel god. The Jews even tried to blend their devotion to God and Molech by going from one place of worship to another. This is plainly described in Ezekiel 23:37–39 which reads: "They committed adultery with their idols; they even sacrificed their children, whom they bore to me, as food for them. They have also done this to me: At that same time they defiled my sanctuary and desecrated my Sabbaths. On the very day they sacrificed their children to their idols, they entered my sanctuary and desecrated it. That is what they did in my house."

One can hardly take it in. The Jews, who once served God, who had brought them into a better land out of slavery in Egypt, and provided for them in many wonderful ways, could now resort to this. They could only have been taken over by demon power. Satan was always nearby, chuckling with glee. The Jews were so confused, so perverted, that they hardly knew whom they worshipped, or how, or why.

A popular place of pagan sacrifice was the valley of Hinnom, from which comes the word "Gehenna" which is the root word for hell (Jer 19:6). What a horrible array of gods!

People really feared these gods. They were so blinded that they really believed these gods were true gods, and many thought that if they did not please these gods they would be destroyed.

It is the same today. Many who are caught up in devil worship in one way or another, are fearful of displeasing the devil and his followers, and this is why many are afraid of giving it all up. It was, and still is, a religion of fear. No, the devil does not discourage religion, he promotes it, and twists it into something horrible and ugly.

The most bewildering case of apostasy in Israel's dark history is that of Solomon. He began well, with a humble prayer for wisdom to enable him to lead the people in truth and love, but in the end he fell victim to Satan's wiles.

Solomon had overwhelming success as king, as long as he served the Lord God with his whole heart. He accumulated 1400 chariots and 12,000 horses. He had riches beyond comprehension; he was greater in riches and wisdom than all the kings in the earth. The whole world sought audience with Solomon, to hear the wisdom that God had put in his heart.

Year by year everyone who came to see him brought a gift: silver and gold, robes, weapons, and spices, horses and mules. Solomon however had one weakness, he loved many foreign women. The Lord had said, " 'You must not intermarry with them, because they will surely turn your heart after their gods.' '' But Solomon held fast to them, he had 700 wives and 300 concubines, and his wives led Solomon astray. He made provision for his wives to worship their gods, and as he grew older he himself went after them; he followed Ashtoreth, the goddess of the Sidonians, and Molech the detestable god of the Ammonites (1 Ki 11:1–5).

Satan always plays on the weaknesses of people. As soon as you let your guard down he is there to tempt and entice you and cause you to sin. Had Solomon cried to God for help in the hour of temptation, the Lord would have helped him to overcome, but we do not read that Solomon did this. Instead, he listened to the devil, just as Eve had done and was deceived. Solomon's position as king, his wealth, and his wisdom, did not make him immune to temptation—these are no safeguards at all. The only safeguard is obedience to God's word, and earnest prayer for strength, courage and power to overcome. Solomon did not repent as David his father had done when he sinned with Bathsheba. If he had repented of his sin, God would have forgiven him, just as he forgave David before him. We read in Psalm 51, the prayer of David, "Wash away all my iniquity and cleanse me from my sin" (verse 2), and "Create in me a pure heart, O God, and renew a steadfast spirit within me" (verse 10).

There are many Psalms in which David testifies to the mercy of God, when he cried to Him for help and strength in the hour of need. There is no temptation put upon us that is more than we can bear, for when we are tempted, God will provide a way out so that we can stand up under it (1 Co 10:13).

It is always sad to see someone who once loved the Lord, now serving the devil, and unrepentant of their sin, with a heart that is cold and hard. We should take heed of the words of Jesus, "'Watch and pray so that you will not fall into temptation. The spirit is willing, but the body is weak'" (Mt 26:41).

Although Satan set up many gods so that the people would worship them instead of God, he could not and never will, overcome those who worship the one true God. Time and time again God gave His people victory in battle against their enemies. The Lord declared by the prophet Isaiah, "Tell the righteous it will be well with them, for they will enjoy the fruit of their deeds. Woe unto the wicked! Disaster is upon them! They will be paid back for what their hands have done" (Isa 3:10–11). We read again in Ecclesiastes 8:12–13, "Although a wicked man commits a hundred crimes and still lives a long time, I know that it will go better with God-fearing men ... because the wicked do not fear God, it will not go well with them, and their days will not lengthen like a shadow." God always rewards those who love Him, and He will give them the victory over all their enemies if they obey Him, and walk in his ways.

Under the influence of Jezebel, the worship of Baal had taken the place of the worship of Jehovah—but Elijah, a prophet of God, challenged 850 prophets of Baal, and got the victory. This is a true story of one man's courage and faith in God, and is a great testimony of victory over evil. But even when Satan sees he has lost, he still persists. What a lesson we can learn from this! If only Christians could be as persistent as this, even when we fail. He doesn't give up so why do we? Satan doesn't age, but his tactics change as we change as a generation of people. He will not give up his plans until the final day when he will be cast into the lake of fire, and all who follow him will go with him.

Satan did his evil work very successfully in Old Testament times. He brought about the downfall of man and the apostasy of a people, not by denying religion, but by perverting it. He did not oppose God's temple in Jerusalem, he merely added to it—a temple of vice for Ashtoreth, a temple of rioting for the Moabite god Chemosh (2 Ki 23:13), and altars of sacrifice for Molech. This was, and still is, the pattern of apostasy, the strategy of Satan. Now there is apostasy in today's religions: Islam, Hinduism, Mormonism, the Jehovah Witnesses and other cults, but also in the established churches such as the Church of England, Catholic, and yes, even in the modern Charismatic churches.

Satan is seeking to overcome people today, as he overcame our first parents, by shaking their confidence in God and leading them to doubt His wisdom, His government, His laws.

Those who have chosen Satan as their leader are not prepared to enter into God's presence. Pride, rebellion, cruelty, deception, disobedience, and other evil diversions are works of Satan to stop men and women from having pure, sweet fellowship with God, through our Lord Jesus Christ.

We carefully secure our homes with locks and keys from those who may seek to harm us, but do we think of the evil one, who is seeking to destroy our soul, who is constantly seeking access to our lives, and against whose attacks we in our own strength, have no method of defence? Those who yield to the claims of

Christ, are always safe under His care, the wicked one cannot break through as long as we are obedient and faithful to Him.

CHAPTER SIX

A way back to God

THE devil, as we have seen, enjoyed a long period of
success; he seemed to hold the whole world in his
sway. In the duration of time between the Old and New
Testaments, Satan was not asleep or inactive, neither
was God asleep, for we read in God's word, that He
never slumbers or sleeps. It was a very pagan world
(except for the Jews' worship of God). There were
witches, sorcerers, and gods of every description, and
every perverted practice imaginable. Far from being
non-religious, seldom had the world been more completely religious. Typified by Athens, the world was
wholly given over to idolatry (Ac 17:16). In New Testament times the Old Testament gods were largely exchanged for new ones, although the old gods were still
there somewhere. The Hellenic culture for example, was
full of deities like Zeus, the supreme god, and Hera, his
wife; Poseidon, god of the sea; Athena, goddess of wisdom and many more. Rome, which occupied Israel in the
lifetime of Jesus, had its assortment of gods, which the
Romans worshipped throughout the whole empire:
Mars, god of war; Apollo, god of literature and healing
(and still very highly regarded by modern-day spiritists);
Quirinus, the state god; Mercury, the messenger of the
gods; Jupiter, the prime god, and many others. Among
the array of gods were an elaborate assortment of goddesses, who seemed to have attributes applicable to
every human circumstance: Juno, wife of Jupiter and
protector of marriage; Ceres, goddess of grain and
plenty; and rising above them all, Cybel, the mother of

gods. Gods of love, still popular today, like the Greek Eros and Roman Cupid, represent the deep longing in the heart of men and women for real love. Goddesses of love, like Venus, Isis, and Aphrodite are still very much esteemed among those who are involved in occult practices.

The devil did his work very thoroughly, he spread his false gods all over the known world. It was into such a world that the promised Messiah was born.

Satan had been warned by God of this event in the garden of Eden, after he successfully deceived Eve, and caused man's fall. The devil was also reminded of it through the prophets of the Old Testament, and I have no doubt he dreaded the dawning of that day.

We read many prophetic promises concerning the birth of Christ in Scripture, ''For to us a child is born, to us a son is given, and the government will be on his shoulders. And he will be called Wonderful Counsellor, Mighty God, Everlasting Father, Prince of Peace'' (Isa 9:6). Other great promises concerning the coming of the Christ to this earth are in Isaiah 53 and 63:1-6, Psalm 22, 68:18, 110 and Jeremiah 23:5-6. These and others shone like stars in the dark night of Hebrew history.

Satan really trembled when the birth of Christ was announced; he knew a way back to God was made for mankind. There was absolutely *nothing* Satan could do about the birth of Christ, for in the fullness of time Christ was born of a virgin in Bethlehem, Judea. Satan then set about trying to kill the Christ child using Herod, the king of Judea as his medium. He filled his heart with anger, and conspired to use the Magi to find the child. But the Magi, who brought gifts and worshipped the child, were warned in a dream not to return to Herod.

When Herod heard that he had been outwitted by the Magi, Satan stirred up even more hatred in his heart, and ordered the slaying of all male children of two years of age and under. This shows yet again the savage side of Satan's already evil nature. Satan delights to cause sorrow, grief and pain.

We do not read much about the childhood of Jesus, apart from the visit to Jerusalem with His earthly parents, when at the age of twelve Christ amazed the teachers in the temple by His understanding. There is no doubt God protected the child, for we read, "Jesus grew in wisdom and stature, and in favour with God and men" (Lk 2:52). This did not please the devil very much, who then planned to oppose Jesus, trick Him, trap Him, and even tried to kill Him before He could complete the work His father sent Him to do, namely, to destroy the works of the devil (1 Jn 3:8).

Christ came to a very pagan world, a world of great evil, a world very much like our world today. Everywhere Christ went, in everything He did and said there was a direct challenge to the devil. He set an example for us to follow, and established for us victory over the forces of darkness. In a world of darkness, Christ was the light. In a world of deceit, Christ was the truth. In a world of great evil, Christ was righteous. In a world of demonic power, Christ was the power of God. Christ's coming to earth signalled a time of direct confrontation with the devil. Satan tempted Christ to forsake His divine purpose, and end the long hard struggle between them. Yet this confrontation was necessary to establish Christ's divine and eternal supremacy over the devil, on earth, as well as in heaven.

Let us look at the first direct confrontation between Christ and the devil. In Mark's Gospel we read, "The Spirit sent him out into the desert" (Mk 1:12), which speaks of Christ's absolute necessity for direct confrontation with the devil, in order to establish and gain mastery over him, once and for all.

They met in the wilderness of Judea, a place so wild, so forbidding, that only the wild beasts lived there. It was a place searing with heat in the daytime and miserably cold at night. Christ had no opportunity to eat; it was only after the forty days had ended, that he was hungry (Lk 4:2).

When the forty days of fasting were ended, the devil took advantage of Christ's physical weakness and hunger to attack His ministry with three subtle temptations.

This is how the devil still works today. When God's children are physically weak, he sees an opportunity to attack them, vex them, and discourage them in every way he can. This is especially true with God's appointed ministers: Satan attacks their ministry for the Lord when circumstances are difficult. The devil tried to lure the Lord into an abuse of His ministry, an abuse of His power and authority and a perversion of His allegiance to His Father.

The first temptation

In the first temptation, Satan struck at a basic human need, suggesting the Lord should turn stones into bread. Listen to what Satan says: '' 'If you are the Son of God, tell these stones to become bread''' (Mt 4:3). Satan tried to plant seeds of doubt into the Lord's mind, concerning His Sonship, just as he planted doubts into Eve's mind in the garden of Eden. Christ answered Satan, '' 'Man does not live on bread alone, but on every word that comes from the mouth of God''' (Mt 4:4). Christ used the same word of God, found in Deuteronomy 8:3. This is our weapon, Jesus set us an example, by using God's word, for His word is sharper than any double-edged sword (Heb 4:12).

Satan hates the word of God, he knows how powerful it is, and how much damage it can do to him and his satanic hosts; so this should encourage us to believe God's word, and use God's word at all times. Hide God's word in your heart, meditate upon it, and you will always get the victory.

The second temptation

The devil then tempted the Lord to leap from the pinnacle of the temple in Jersualem, making an irrelevant use of Scripture to assure Christ he would be safe. Once again the devil tempted Jesus to resort to sensationalism as a means of demonstrating His power over all other powers. The devil is very clever; he can use Scripture to try and confuse the child of God. He can make them take Scripture out of its context. Notice here that Christ said "It is written" in answer to the devil's first temptation, and the devil comes back with the same words that Christ used: " 'If you are the Son of God, throw yourself down. *For it is written*: "He will command his angels concerning you, and they will lift you up in their hands, so that you will not strike your foot against a stone." ' Jesus answered him, '*It is also written*: "Do not put the Lord your God to the test" ' " (Mt 4:6–7). Christ teaches us that even while He was tempted, tired and hungry, one scripture does not contradict another.

The third temptation

Satan's last assault on the divinity of Christ was so blatant, so overt, so specific in its aim it almost defies belief. The devil actually suggested that Christ should bow down and worship him (Mt 4:9). Satan showed Christ all the kingdoms of the world and their splendour, and said, " 'All this I will give you, if you will bow down and worship me.' " There was a particularly subtle side to this temptation: by yielding to it, the devil implied that Jesus could have dominion over the whole world without going through the agony of Gethsemane, the humiliation of the judgment hall, and the suffering of Calvary. Satan tried to tempt Jesus to take a short cut to His dominion, to bypass His death by crucifixion.

The deep implication of this temptation is too terrible to consider. If Christ had failed the test it would have eliminated the only way back to God, the only way by which we can be saved. It is the blood of Christ, shed on Calvary's cross, that provides a way back to God, and salvation for the whole human race. If Christ had failed the test, He would have abandoned mankind to certain death. But let us rejoice that Christ did not abandon mankind, He overcame temptation, and made a way back to God for us.

When we look at the last temptation alongside the devil's desire to usurp God, we see again that the original ambition of Satan has never been abandoned: he still seeks worship. In the last days we shall see him increasingly seeking worship for himself by perverting the true worship of God.

After the wilderness ordeal, we read that the devil departed from Jesus until an opportune time (Lk 4:13). Although we do not read of any further face-to-face encounters there are numerous descriptions of other confrontations. For example, Jesus came upon many demoniacs and cast demons out of them. The gospels are full of accounts of Christ's liberation or healing of the demon-possessed, some of which are worth mentioning, because they provide proof of Christ's spiritual authority. In Mark 5:1–20 we read how Christ and His disciples encountered a man in the regions of Gadara whose demon-possession was very severe; he wore no clothes, he lived among the tombs and no-one could tame him. Night and day he cut himself with stones, and it seemed that everyone was afraid of him. He saw Jesus coming from a distance and fell on his knees in front of Him, and shouted at the top of his voice, "What do you want with me, Jesus, Son of the Most High God? Swear to God that you won't torture me." Jesus asked his name, and the man replied, "My name is Legion, for we are many." Jesus commanded the demons to come out of the man. In the Roman militia a legion was a force of three to six thousand soldiers. As the term was used to refer to the demoniac, it meant that this man was possessed by multiple demons. When Jesus cast them out they begged Him to be sent into a herd of pigs; Jesus gave permission, and the demons entered the pigs, which ran down a steep slope into the sea and were drowned. The man who had been possessed then sat at the feet of Jesus, clothed, and in his right mind. I do not doubt that Satan, who had this poor man bound for so long, was absolutely furious.

Christ's authority over the spirit world was further demonstrated in other cases, as when Peter, James and John met a demoniac on their way down from the Mount of Transfiguration (Mk 9:14–27). Just like the man who was possessed with multiple demons, this boy had numerous maladies as a result of demon-possession, and his father said that the evil spirit threw the boy into convulsions, he foamed at the mouth, gnashed his teeth, and became rigid. The father was very distressed, and brought the boy to Jesus' disciples. They could not cast the evil spirit out, but Jesus cast the demon out and the boy rose up from the ground where the demon had thrown him. He was cured, delivered, free, and the people were amazed at the mighty power of God (Lk 9:43).

Neither the number nor the nature of the demons mattered to Jesus; He was master of every enemy power. Jesus exercised authority over them. Frequently the demons recognised Jesus, with such words as these: "'You are the Son of God'" (Mk 3:11). Jesus ordered the demons to be silent. He would not allow demons to announce His deity.

Jesus went about doing good. He healed the sick, gave sight to the blind, cleansed the leper and set free the demon-possessed. Satan was just a bystander; he could not do a thing about it. Everyone was attracted to Jesus. His compassion accepted people, His power healed people, and Satan's power was to put to flight.

Christ had authority over death—the greatest and the most dreaded power of all. Death is the final truth that we all must face, death is the consequence of sin, the fruit of rebellion that reaches back to Satan's deception of Eve in the garden of Eden. Now Jesus Christ manifested His power over death by restoring the dead to life. He raised at least three people from the dead: the widow's son in Nain (Lk 7:11–15),

Lazarus in Bethany (Jn 11:11–44), and the daughter of Jairus (Mt 9:18–26).

Christ had authority over sin. Christ's forgiveness of sin was the rescue of souls from the bondage of the devil, an action so bold that even the religious leaders were astonished by it. They questioned His authority, or rather Satan through them dared to question it: "Why does this fellow talk like that? He's blaspheming! Who can forgive sins but God alone?" (Mk 2:7).

Christ demonstrated His authority to forgive sins when he forgave the woman caught in the act of adultery (Jn 8:3–11). The religious leaders of that day laid a trap for Jesus by bringing the woman to him (supposedly for advice and judgment). This was a direct challenge to Christ's authority, another of Satan's attacks on the Lord's Sonship, working through these so-called religious leaders, who were nothing but hypocrites themselves. Jesus resolved this confrontation by writing on the ground, which exposed the sins of these hypocritical leaders, who were the woman's accusers. They left one by one, and the woman was left alone with Jesus, who said, "Woman, where are your accusers? Has anyone condemned you?" "No-one sir," she said. "Then neither do I condemn you. Go now and leave your life of sin." Satan was defeated yet again.

Christ had authority over the elements. Jesus and the Father were one. Christ was with God in the beginning, and the world was made by Him, therefore He had authority over that which He had made. Jesus said to Philip, " 'Don't you believe that I am in the Father, and that the Father is in me? The words I say to you are not just my own. Rather, it is the Father living in me, who is doing His work' " (Jn 14:10).

On one occasion Jesus was in a small boat on the lake of Galilee, and a sudden very fierce storm arose. The disciples were with Him in the boat. They were experienced fishermen, and knew the moods of the sea but they were unable to cope, and cried to the Lord who was asleep, "Teacher, don't you care if we drown?" He arose, and rebuked the wind and waves, and there was a great calm (Mk 4:35-39).

I believe this was yet another time the devil tried unsuccessfully to get rid of the Lord before He could die on the cross. What better opportunity than when the Lord was asleep in a boat, in the middle of the sea? But even the wind and waves obeyed Him (Mk 4:41).

On another occasion Jesus walked on water (Jn 6:16-21). The disciples were afraid when they saw Jesus walking on the water towards them, but the Lord said, "'It is I, don't be afraid'" (Jn 6:20).

Jesus invested His disciples with His own power and authority. In Luke 9:1 we read, "When Jesus had called the Twelve together, he gave them power and authority to drive out all demons and to cure diseases." Satan not only attacked the Lord, he attacked the disciples, and he still does today.

The greatest opposition Christ encountered came from the religious leaders: the Scribes, Pharisees and Sadducees. The Pharisees had once been an honourable body of men, whose name means "the separated ones". They who had once been worthy, who for so long awaited the coming of the Messiah, they who had once kept Judaism fit for His coming, were now not fit themselves when He did come. They followed the pattern of apostasy by ministering error mixed with truth, by substituting self-righteousness for true righteousness and by crushing the spirit of the law with the letter of the law. The devil had so successfully infiltrated this proud sect, that even the harlots, drunkards, tax collectors and thieves were more sympathetic to Jesus than they were (Mt 21:31). This proud sect committed the ultimate blasphemy when they accused the Lord of casting out devils through Beelzebub the chief of devils (Lk 11:15).

Jesus asserted truth without hesitation, and was very strong in His opposition to these pretentious religious leaders, criticising them with boldness (Mt 5:20). Christ asserted truth because error must always be silenced with truth, and the power of wrong must be overcome with the power of righteousness. Christ overcame the devil in every situation, and by doing so he staked a position for His children, and showed us the way to attain it.

When the seventy-two returned, whom the Lord had sent before him to every place He himself would go later, they said, " 'Lord, even the demons submit to us in your name.' " Jesus replied, " 'I saw Satan fall like lightning from heaven' " (Lk 10:17–18). Jesus saw Satan cast out of heaven long before these men, or anyone else, encountered him, so Jesus knew just what He was up against here on the earth.

Jesus said these wonderful words to His disciples, " 'I have given you authority to trample on snakes and scorpions and to overcome all the power of the enemy; nothing will harm you. However, do not rejoice that the spirits submit to you, but rejoice that your names are written in heaven' " (Lk 10:19).

Just as Jesus recognised the devil, so can we. By the power of the Holy Spirit, we can discern what is of the devil, and what is of the Lord; between right and wrong, true and false. It is entirely up to us to use the power He has given us, and resist the devil, and then he will flee from us (Jas 4:7).

The Lord preached good news to the poor, He proclaimed freedom for the prisoners, and the recovery of sight to the blind, release for those who are oppressed, and proclaimed the year of the Lord's favour (Lk 4:18–19).

Everywhere He went He was a blessing: the sick were healed, the blind received their sight, the lame walked, the deaf heard, and those who were bound by Satan were released. But Jesus also came to die for the sins of the whole world. When Jesus tried to teach the disciples that the Son of Man must suffer many things, to be rejected by the elders, the chief priests and teachers of the law, they did not understand—especially Peter, who took Jesus aside and rebuked Him. Jesus knew instantly that Satan was speaking through Peter, and He rebuked Satan, saying, " 'Get behind me,

Satan! . . . you do not have in mind the things of God, but the things of men' '' (Mt 16:23).

The time was approaching for Jesus to be brought before Pilate to be tried, and the disciples forsook Him and fled. They could not even stay awake and pray in the Lord's darkest hour in the garden of Gethsemane, where He prayed and agonised and sweat great drops of blood (Lk 22:44). The battle was fought and won right there in the garden of Gethsemane, where Christ prayed to His Father and asked His Father if it was possible for that hour to pass from Him. He prayed, '' 'Father, if you are willing, take this cup from me; yet not my will, but yours be done.' '' Christ was willing to pay the debt of sin; He was willing to be crucified for us, that we might go free.

Satan then filled Peter's heart with great fear and he denied the Lord he loved three times with curses, saying, '' 'I don't know him' '' (Lk 22:54–62). Satan must have gloated over this at the time, but later Peter repented and wept bitterly, and that silenced Satan for a while.

This was the time that Satan dreaded the most, and if he trembled when Jesus was born, he trembled even more when Christ, the Son of God, was made sin for us at the cross of Calvary, because Satan was defeated at the cross where Jesus shed His blood, so that men and women could be saved. Satan suffered a massive blow when the veil of the temple was torn in two, from top to bottom, for it meant that a way back to God was made for sinners. Yes! Satan knew that the prophecies concerning the Messiah were fulfilled, and the supreme and perfect sacrifice for sin was made and now mankind could come again and have pure and sweet fellowship with God. This little chorus that I learned in Sunday school many years ago puts it very simply and plainly:

There's a way back to God from the dark paths of sin,
There's a door that is open, and you may go in.
At Calvary's cross is where you begin,
When you come as a sinner to Jesus.

We read with reverence and awe how Jesus suffered all the agony in the garden of Gethsemane, all the humiliation of the judgment hall, and the terrible suffering of the cross. All that Satan tried to tempt Him to bypass, Jesus willingly endured so that mankind could be reconciled to God. The scene of Calvary was a powerful sight, a heart-rending sight. How anyone can read the accounts leading up to His crucifixion, and the crucifixion itself without being deeply moved is beyond comprehension. We read in Matthew 27:51–53, "At that moment the curtain of the temple was torn in two from top to bottom. The earth shook and the rocks split. The tombs broke open and the bodies of many holy people who had died were raised to life. They came out of the tombs, and after Jesus' resurrection they went into the holy city and appeared to many people."

When Christ rose from the dead he triumphed over the grave, he triumphed over death, showing plainly that He was victorious over the devil. The devil must have been really shaken, because he knew that those who had been in his dreadful grip for so long could be freed, and receive the gift of everlasting life.

How the disciples rejoiced to see their beloved Master alive! He appeared first to Mary Magdalene, one of Satan's former slaves, whom Christ set free from seven evil spirits (and that was before He went to the cross). Now Christ had conquered death so that men and women who trust Him as Saviour will never die. At one time Christ spoke these words to Martha, the sister of Mary and Lazarus whom Christ raised from the dead, "'I am the resurrection and the life. He who believes in me will live, even though he dies; and whoever lives and believes in me will never die'" (Jn 11:25–26). How those words thrill us today!

When Christ died and rose again, He took the keys of death away from Satan, He descended into the lowest parts of the earth, He led captives with Him, and ascended on high (Eph 4:8–10). Can you imagine how Satan felt when Jesus did this? Not only did Satan fail to stop Christ dying on the cross for lost and sinful man,

Christ released captives; the dead saints arose from their graves and Jesus took the keys of death and hell away from Satan. What a massive defeat all this was for the devil! In Revelation 1:18 we read, ''I am the Living One; I was dead, and behold I am alive for ever and ever! And I hold the keys of death and Hades.'' I can just imagine the look on Satan's face when Jesus Christ, the Son of God, took the keys of death straight out of his ugly blood-stained hands. This scene really excites me. My Jesus, so mighty, so powerful, looks Satan straight in the eyes and pronounces his power over death, and takes away the devil's authority over death, in the devil's domain. What a sight that must have been!

Satan, powerful as he may seem, is not *all powerful*. Satan does not hold the keys of death, Christ does, and no-one can die, neither saint nor sinner, unless Christ permits it to happen. What a revelation! What an eternal truth! How very wonderful it is!

What Satan had robbed man of in the garden of Eden, Christ, the second Adam, through His death and resurrection, had restored, to those who own Him as Lord and Saviour. For since death came through a man (Adam), the resurrection of the dead comes also through a man (Jesus). For as in Adam all die, so in Christ all will be made alive.

When Christ arose from the dead, Satan re-organised his army of demons to devise another plan in order to divert men and women from accepting Christ, who said, '' 'I am the way and the truth and the life. No-one comes to the Father except through me.' '' (Jn 14:6).

One of Satan's first diversions was to tell people that Christ did not rise from the dead, that Jesus Christ was still in the tomb. The chief priests and elders were alarmed when they heard the news that Christ had risen from the dead and had been seen by many. They bribed the soldiers with a large sum of money to tell the people that the disciples had come and stolen the body of Jesus by night, and this story circulated among the Jews (Mt 28:11–15).

This lie has been passed on into even our generation. There are a great many people who do not believe in the resurrection of Christ, and sad to say, even some in the church who have said the same thing. This is just a clever trick of the devil, who knows his time is short, and still desires to destroy men and women and take them to hell with him. It is very convenient for the devil because he knows that by telling this lie, men would say, "Jesus Christ is dead, so He cannot change me." Some people just do not want any changes in their lives, it is easier for them to hold on to their sin. A great many people know that Jesus is alive, because they also know that a dead Christ could not change them, only a risen glorified Saviour can do this, and He is still changing lives today. He changed me!

It matters not how Satan diverts people today, as long as they are diverted from the foot of the cross. The devil caters for every class of society, and all modern trends. We will be looking at some of these diversions in the following chapters.

CHAPTER SEVEN

Devilish diversions

SATAN is always ready to supply the heart's desires, and to palm off deception in the place of truth. Not everyone would believe the lie that Christ had not risen from the dead, there was too much evidence to the contrary, "The Lord added to their number daily those who were being saved" (Ac 2:47). Very often though, people who throw up their hands in horror at one deception will readily believe another, so what better for Satan than to raise up false doctrines, and cause confusion and division?

In Revelation the devil is repeatedly referred to as a deceiver: "Satan, which deceiveth the whole world" (Rev 12:9 AV). "He deceived the inhabitants of the earth" (Rev 13:14). The truth is, that Satan has been a deceiver from the beginning, is now, and will be till the end.

Satan panders to the heart's desires, inclinations and weaknesses of his prey. The world is full of people who are willing to be deceived, as long as the deception is pleasant and fulfilling, if only for a short time. Satan's scheme is to conquer the cause of Christ by means of division, duplication, and diversion.

Satan knows that when there is division in the Church of God, the whole body of believers are weak and defenceless. Satan can then say to the outsider, "Christians are always quarrelling among themselves." Paul speaks of this in 1 Corinthians 3:3–4: "You are still worldly. For since there is jealousy and quarrelling among you, are you not worldly? . . . For when one says, 'I follow Paul,' and another, 'I follow Apollos,' are you not mere men?'' Paul speaks of this again in Romans 16:17–18, ''I urge you, brothers, to watch out for those who cause divisions and put obstacles in your way that are contrary to the teaching you have learned. Keep away from them. For such people are not serving our Lord Christ, but their own appetites. By smooth talk and flattery they deceive the minds of naive people.''

Who is behind all divisions in the house of the Lord? No-one else but the devil himself! Much is said in the world today about divisions in the church, and much is said about the breakdown of morals, and this is appropriate for these should be guarded lest Christian integrity be lost altogether. But there are other breakdowns which are just as important and threaten the cause of Christ in our world: the breakdown of fellowship, faith, confidence and love. When there are breakdowns of personal relationships within the church, the body of believers are weak, and nothing invites the attacks of Satan more than schism and division. When Christians devour each other with suspicion, jealousy and backbiting, they are doing the devil's work for him. In 1 Peter 5:8 we read, ''Be self-controlled and alert. Your enemy the devil prowls around like a roaring lion looking for someone to devour.'' When we on the other hand, love one another and build one another up, the whole world will know that we are genuine; we read this in God's word, ''All men will know that you are my disciples, if you love one another'' (Jn 13:35).

Divisions are nothing but clever diversions of the devil to stop Christians from doing what we should be doing: loving the Lord with all our hearts, minds, and spirits, and reaching out to the lost with a message of hope, love, and salvation through the shed blood of Christ, God's Son.

Diversion is another clever tactic of the devil in his warfare against the church of Jesus Christ. Diversion is the focussing of attention on one matter whilst another of greater importance passes unnoticed. There are many hundreds of diversions today that negate important issues, that lead away from Christ and His plan of salvation, and we are going to focus on just a few of them.

Duplication is probably the worst of Satan's diversionary tactics. It is certainly the most confusing to many people, and the surest way to victory for the devil. What Satan cannot deny, he imitates, and obtains the same result as with a successful denial. The adverse effect of duplication is clearly illustrated by the metaphor of a sudden influx of bogus money. The flood of counterfeit notes creates suspicion of the genuine article. It works the same way with Christianity. The counterfeit version causes suspicion and confusion, which in the end leads to an outright rejection. The devil is very busy supplying false Christs and false religion, which is just what he did in the Old Testament, only now it is centred around Christ, rather than God.

Jesus warned the disciples that false Christs would appear. Mark 13:21–22: ''At that time if anyone says to you, 'Look, here is the Christ!' or, 'Look, there he is!' do not believe it. For false Christs and false prophets will appear and perform signs and miracles to deceive the elect—if that were possible.'' Let us take a look at some of the false Christs, and false doctrines that Satan has raised up. Some of these false Christs have claimed they were Christ reincarnated, and others have said they were Christ himself returned to the earth.

Father Divine

This was the assumed name of the leader of an American Messianic movement that was strong in the 1930s to the 1960s. He lived in a New York mansion, which his devoted followers gave him, in the lap of luxury, until he died in 1965. He claimed he was Christ, and many hundreds believed him.

Children of God

In 1968, a Christian and Missionary Alliance minister, named David Berg, began an outreach among the hippies. He recruited many hundreds who assisted him. They gave up possessions, they left family and friends, schools and jobs to live in communes, and shared all things in common. Things went very wrong when Berg started to teach false doctrine, and things got too hot for him, so he kept moving around. The movement soon spread to England, bringing yet more error and deceit. Berg assumed the identities of Moses and David, king of Israel. His vulgar letters, which he called MO letters, MO being short for Moses, were, according to him, God's word for today, as compared with the Bible, which now became God's word for yesterday. In addition to having all things in common, Berg and his followers began to share wives and husbands, and began to offer free sex for new converts, calling it "flirty fishing." This is so tragic, because it all got even worse. Those who started out with a genuine desire to serve the Lord, were deceived into following this man, Berg, who led them far away from the truth, into almost unbelievable perversions. They started out with the name "Children of God", but were in fact far from doing God's work, and are now doing the work of the devil. Later on they changed their name to "the family of love"—but what kind of love? They were diverted from the right path, and trod the path of wickedness.

Hare Krishna Society

When members of this cult first began their recruiting activities in this country, it was looked upon as a huge joke. Surely we send missionaries to the Orient to convert people from paganism, not them to us! Wearing Oriental garb and with shaven heads, they peddle their literature and articles to finance their movement. They can be seen at airports, bus-stations, and sometimes the main shopping centres, dancing around and chanting some mumbo-jumbo, which is often a source of amusement to passers-by. The main teaching of this cult is that Krishna is a personal god and present in any form he chooses: in wood, stone, marble, and in the things made by his followers. Krishna is also present in people, and has been for 5000 years or more. Although Krishna is the official god, Swami Prabhupada the guru of the cult, is also given god-like devotion by his followers. Here we see that Satan uses the element of mystery. People are drawn to something that looks, or seems mysterious or spooky, something different, which attracts people, especially young people, who go through a stage of being generally bored and discontented with their lives. Satan, the greatest deceiver of all time has certainly deceived many people by this awful cult.

The Unification Church

This is yet another cult that came from the Far East, and its adherents are widely known as ''The Moonies''. Sun Myung Moon is of Presbyterian background, but has strayed far away from his Christian roots. The Moonies follow a creed that is a pot-pourri of Biblical teaching, Oriental philosophy, and the personal views of Sun Myung Moon. New converts are won through an aggressive recruitment programme. The Moonies operate under numerous related organisations and raise funds by selling flowers they have grown on their land, and making candles, and they call their methods ''heavenly deception''. Deception it is, but heavenly it is *not*. They practise communal living, in common with most cults, but they have the added flourish of mass marriages of couples, who have been personally paired off by Moon himself. The Moonies have attracted much attention from the international press because of their rigid rules which, when investigated amount to nothing else but brain-washing. Followers are compelled to forsake all to follow Moon: family, friends and jobs. Many have given their property, houses and cars to the movement, and many distressed parents have tried to win their teenage children back. Some have been successful, others have not. Altogether, it is a heart-breaking fact that the Moonies have been responsible for causing the break-up of families, who have never been the same since.

Moon speaks of a trinity of religions: Judaism, Christianity, and the Unification Church, and believes that there should be a religious-political movement, with him as the leader, of course. His followers believe that he is the Messiah, a belief that Moon does not discourage. He often speaks of the so-called mistakes of Jesus, such as His failure to use political power to build a material empire. Moon in the late 80s had a worldwide following of 60,000 members, and well over 10,000 workers, with a total following (as distinct from membership) of more than three million in the United States alone; although there has been a break away from the movement since the exposure of the financial swindle it was mixed up in some years ago.

The Moonies and Hare Krishna are just the tip of the iceberg of false religions; there are many more major and minor cults in our world today. They include such movements as Divine Light Mission, The Church of Scientology, Eckankar, the faith of Total Awareness, and a host of others. Most of the cults are fairly obvious to most mature Christians, but let us not forget those others which, because of the fact that they are well-known to the general public, are often overlooked, and therefore often escape exposure. We are going to have a fresh look at the more well-known cults.

Jehovah's Witnesses

The operations and the literature of the ''Jehovah's Witnesses'' have spread into 160 countries, and they are still expanding. That there is a huge and efficient organisation behind the movement is evidenced by the vast coverage of its literature. The founder was Charles Taze Russell, of Pittsburg USA. Finding no existing religion to his liking, he assumed the title ''Pastor'' and founded one of his own, the most attractive feature of which was the non-existence of hell. He became increasingly popular in his denunciation of organised religion and the clergy.

Mr Russell prophesied that our churches, schools, banks and governments would be completely destroyed by October 1914. Later, when it did not happen as he said, the destruction was promised in instalments ending in 1925. Here are some of their errors: denial of the Trinity; Christ was created and not Divine until His resurrection; He was merely a human atonement and His body was not raised from the dead; His second advent took place in 1874, and the saints were raised in 1878; there is no personal Holy Spirit; the Lord is now a purely spirit being; the Christian church was rejected by God in 1878; there is a second probation for the wicked.

Christians are told that their way, and their church is wrong, and only the Witnesses are right. The door-to-door workers are very highly trained and know just what Scriptures to refer to, which are cleverly twisted to confound the unwary. It is wise to know just how they do twist the Scriptures and take them out of context. They will not stay with you long if they think they are in danger of being caught out themselves.

They try very hard to get inside your home for a Bible study—which is always taken from their own version of the Bible. Here Satan takes advantage of lonely people who have let these people enter their homes, confusing their minds regarding Christianity by telling them their way is the only way of truth. Often they get their converts through (what they call) Bible study in their homes. Christians who have been let down and hurt by the church in one way or another are also the people they pursue, and the Jehovah's Witnesses have been known to call back time and time again in order to win them over. Here we see the devil at work among those who have left the church, playing upon their emotions. We see the craftiness of the enemy telling people that all churches are wrong, and all churches have failed. Some Christians have not received the right counsel, or none at all, and some have been rejected by the church, which again is the work of the devil.

People just cannot understand that some of our churches have grown cold and are not preaching the truth, but the fact is, this is just the place where the devil seeks entry to drive people away from God and lead them into error. It is vital therefore that the Christian church should hold fast to the truth, in preaching the truth, caring for the flock, and always being watchful and alert, with prayer, and loving counsel for those who are troubled, giving the devil no opportunity to gain a foothold.

The Mormons

Mormonism, or the church of Jesus Christ of the Latter Day Saints, is yet another false cult that specialises in door-to-door work, with a membership in 1960 of 1,650,000 in all its branches. Magnificent and costly Mormon temples have been erected in places as widely separate as Los Angeles and New Zealand. Their story is that Joseph Smith, an illiterate young man, who was hardly able to read until manhood and knew practically nothing of the Bible, had an angelic visitor in 1823. This angelic visitor, Moroni by name, revealed to Smith that, in 420 AD, there had been secreted in the hill Cumorah, near Palmra, New York, several golden plates on which were inscribed the history of the Nephites, who came to America from Jerusalem in 600 BC. Joseph Smith went to the spot, and there were the golden plates and a large pair of spectacles, which he called "Urim and Thummin", and by the aid of which he was able to decipher and translate into English the mystic hieroglyphics, which he claimed were "reformed Egyptian".

All this so-called new revelation resulted in the *Book of Mormon*. The degree of credulity required to accept the Mormon version of the origin of their supposedly holy book seems inexplicable, unless it be that "because they refused to love the truth and so be saved . . . God sends them a powerful delusion so that they will believe the lie'' (2 Th 2:10–11).

If it is asked why Mormonism should be classed as a heresy, the answer is three-fold. Firstly it is anti-Christian. While concealing its errors under the terminology of Christianity, it either perverts or denies all fundamental truths of Christianity, for instance

1. Christ's atonement has only to do with the sins of Adam.
2. Christ is the Son of Adam, God, and Mary, not born of a Virgin.
3. The Holy Spirit is a divine fluid.

All these points are substantiated in their teaching (*Cults and Isms*, J.O. Saunders, Lakeland (1984), p. 109).

Secondly, polygamy was practised among Mormons, at least from the time of the first public announcement of the doctrine in Utah in 1852. It is true that, after a legal battle, the practice was officially abandoned in 1889, but it has been sporadically indulged in until a date as recent as 1944, when law enforcement officers arrested 46 members of the fundamental sect of Mormons in Utah, Idaho and Arizona. It was reported in an interview, ''Of course we believe in what we are doing; this is far bigger than the individual, for it will encompass much more than the man-made laws by which the world lives, and will become a fundamental component in the lives of all righteous living people.'' Here are Joseph Smith's words, from the 1944 edition of *Doctrines and Covenants*: ''If any man espouse a virgin, and desire to espouse another, and the first give her consent, and if he espouse the second, and they are virgins, and have bowed to no man, then he is justified, he cannot commit adultery, for they are given to him.'' All this in spite of such scriptures as, ''The overseer must be above reproach, the husband of but one wife'' and ''A deacon must be the husband of but one wife'' (1 Ti 3:2,12).

While the reorganised Mormon church repudiates polygamy, even they cannot deny that it was practised by all their original twelve apostles. The very fact that polygamy was tolerated at any stage amongst Mormons is sufficient to condemn the whole Mormon system.

Thirdly, Mormons have a counterfeit Bible, the *Book of Mormon*, the origin of which is doubtful and suspicious. They believe the Bible to be the word of God, so far as it is correctly translated, but they say they also believe the *Book of Mormon* to be the word of God. To the Mormons the Bible is not the sole and infallible word of God, it is just a tool to further their subtle teachings. This is what they say concerning the Bible: ''If it be that the Apostles and the Evangelists wrote the books of the New Testament, that does not mean they were divinely inspired at the time they were written.'' Furthermore, ''Wilford Woodruff is a prophet, and he can make more scriptures as good as those in the Bible'' (Apostle J. W. Taylor Conference, Salt Lake City, April 1897). And about the writings of Joseph Smith, ''His literary labours must not be forgotten, he produced more scriptures than any other man we have on record.''

We are clearly warned in Revelation 22:18 about adding to God's word: ''I warn everyone who hears the words of the prophecy of this book: If anyone adds anything to them, God will add to him the plagues described in this book.'' The same applies to those who take away words from the Bible: ''If anyone takes words away from this book of prophecy, God will take away from him his share in the tree of life and in the holy city, which are described in this book'' (Rev 22:19).

The whole of the teachings of the Mormons are blasphemous, yet the outward appearance of those who knock at the doors is clean and upright, which proves the devil does indeed appear as ''an angel of light'' and deceives many today. The command of the Scriptures is clear, ''From such turn aside''. We are warned about deceitful workers in 2 Corinthians 11:13, ''For such men are false apostles, deceitful workmen, masquerading as apostles of Christ.''

This collective confusion of cults is Satan's handiwork.

It provides a fertile field for him, and imposes great difficulty for the true church of God. One thing is very clear, the devil is not anti-religious, only anti-Christian. The devil has provided a massive supermarket of false religions for the last days, and people who are lonely and hungry for love and acceptance are buying. It's all part and parcel of the clever diversion away from the foot of the old rugged cross and the simple way of salvation through Jesus Christ, and the diversions are varied and many.

Let it be emphasised again that the devil, choosing duplication from among his deceitful works, has flooded the world with every conceivable religion, in order to confuse the followers of Christ, and those who are earnestly seeking the truth. He has mixed true with lies, and it is often difficult to know what is true and what is false. The only safeguard is the written word of God. Stray from it, or put your own interpretation upon it, and you are heading for danger, deceit and error.

This also goes for diversions which are already in the Christian churches. Although many would not believe me, or agree with me, I have to speak the truth, without fear of what men think or say. I have seen great error creeping into our churches. The subtle part about it all is that it creeps in very *slowly*, and no-one sees it at first. Let me state emphatically that I believe every word of the Bible is truth, but I have seen the truths of God's word exaggerated beyond truth, until the precious truth of His word is lost. For example, I believe in the gifts of the spirit, and believe these gifts are for the church today, but the devil has even tried to distort these with false manifestations. I have heard false tongues, and false prophecy in the church, but these are not easily discerned even by the true child of God, so it is vital that we discern aright, and deal with this in a proper way.

Let me give you an example of the false gift of discernment of spirits. This has happened on several occasions, and if I did not myself have the true gift of discernment of spirits, it could have greatly upset me or discouraged me, which is just what the devil planned. I was speaking in several churches, giving my testimony, and teaching on spiritual warfare when someone came to me and said, "I discern sister that you are still in bondage to witchcraft." Knowing this was a lie, I replied, "What makes you say such a thing?" "Because I have the gift of discernment," she said. "There is no such gift," I answered her, "I am not in bondage to witchcraft at all, or what would I be doing here warning about it? I also have the gift you say you have, but it is not called the gift of discernment, it is called the gift of *discernment of spirits*. This lady, and others who have tried through the enemy of souls, to stop my ministry, have sadly been deceived by the great deceiver himself. Let me also share with you something else that happened to me not very long ago.

For some time I have not been in the best of health, and although I have been prayed for, I have not been fully healed. This has not worried me as much as it has worried other people, who have tried in their own strength to do something about it. Some have said to me, "I discern that you are bitter, and that is why you are not healed." Others have said to me, "You are resisting the Holy Spirit." And again others have stated, "There is unconfessed sin in your life." All this can be very upsetting to someone who is ill, and knows full-well that the things they are saying are not true. The so-called revelation from God these people gave to me are always the answers that are given when they themselves have run out of answers. When Christian people do not receive healing the way they think they should, they blame the person who needs healing. When I did not fall down on the floor, as many others did, and get up healed, it seemed to offend them. How very careful we should be! The devil seeks to pull down, to discourage, to harm, to damage the Christian's faith, to make the word of God, and the gifts of the spirit look suspicious, and even stupid.

Another trick of the devil concerning the Christian church is to bring into the church false prophets who are readily accepted as true prophets of God by the leaders of the church.

This is because the leaders are ignorant of the Scriptures as to how the devil is working today. Many dear children of God have been in deep despair because of false prophecies. When someone prophesies over you and brings condemnation upon you in front of a congregation, that is not from God, because God does not work like that. The devil is an accuser of the children of God, and will do all in his power to bring condemnation upon them. We read in God's word, ''Therefore, there is now no condemnation for those who are in Christ Jesus . . . who do not live according to the sinful nature but according to the Spirit'' (Ro 8:1,4).

There is also a spirit of entertainment creeping into the church where the word of God takes second place to music. Music has a very important place in the worship of God, so it is to be expected that the devil will try to pervert this, and put in its place music to entertain, rather than edify, the church of God. When prayer and worship, and the preaching of the word of God takes second place to music, singing, and dancing, then something is very wrong. When singing and dancing and other forms of entertainment take up most of the service, and the preaching of the word of God and prayer takes only 20 minutes at the most, then something must be wrong somewhere. When so-called men of God take more time begging for money than they do preaching the word of God, and praying for those in need, then something is wrong. Although it seems that God is blessing them when the money flows in, the devil is laughing his head off, because he sees how easy it is to deceive many people, even in the church.

There are precious people sitting in our congregations, in great need of healing, those in need of deliverance from bondage, and indeed, who are unconverted, and those in need of counselling in many areas—the list is endless; and there is not even an invitation to go forward for prayer in order to get their needs met, or to talk to someone about their needs. It seems tragic to me. There seems to be a lack of compassion for a lost and dying world, and God will judge His people for this.

What is needed today more than ever before, is the repentance of God's people: for the absence of real compassion, the lack of conviction of sin, and the lack of the power and presence of the Holy Spirit. Coldness, apathy, disregard for the truth, worldliness, loss of vision, lack of power, loss of courage, teaching and instruction from God's word—all this, and much more, is an opening for bringing in further diversions of the devil into the church of Jesus Christ. We must be watchful and alert, prayerful and wise, powerful in the Holy Spirit, humble and true, always abounding in the work of the Lord, seeking to do His will, and building His church, as Christ has commanded us to do. Jesus is building His church today, despite the devil's attempts to tear down and destroy, but this does not excuse us from playing our part, to prevent this from happening.

There is no time to waste. Christ is coming soon. It is time to wake up from the sleep of carelessness, and repent, so that the Lord can pour out His Spirit upon His people, and to hasten the times of refreshing and growth. To meet the needs of this and other lands, there is a need for Holy Ghost revival, and it starts in the house of God. The devil will do his utmost to stop revival and keep God's people in darkness and bondage. The preaching of the word of God under the anointing of the Holy Spirit, is the only way that the conviction of sin will fall upon the hearers, and the devil will be overcome and defeated in his intentions towards the church of Christ today.

This is God's promise to His people, ''If my people, who are called by my name, will humble themselves and pray and seek my face and turn from their wicked ways, then will I hear from heaven and will forgive their sin and will heal their land'' (2 Ch 7:14).

Keep two things in mind. First, behind every scheme of Satan there is a determination to pervert true worship, and replace it with his own; this is the intention behind all apostasy. Second, the deceptive traps of Satan pose no danger to those who keep their place in Christ and shun evil whenever or however it appears.

When we know who we are in Christ and we are not ignorant of the devil's devices, we will be safe—for the loving Saviour knows how to keep His own. But those who nibble at the traps of Satan, as a mouse nibbles at the cheese in the trap, will be caught in that trap. Those who play with fire will be burned; but those who keep their eyes on Jesus, and walk in His ways, He will keep them in perfect peace until He comes or calls.

CHAPTER EIGHT

The sanctuaries of Satan

ALONG with false Christs and false prophets, there is now an added dimension of deceit: the revival of the practice and belief in occult practices. Judging by the way Satan is wheeling out all his big guns to use against the church, he is apparently getting really desperate. In the book of Revelation we read just what his intensity will be like in the last days: "Woe to the inhabiters of the earth and of the sea! For the devil is come down unto you, having great wrath, because he knoweth that he hath but a short time" (Rev 12:12 AV).

Witchcraft, satanism, spiritism and other black arts were with us long before the flood and were forbidden, first to the Jews, and then to the Christians. As the children of Israel drew near to Canaan, where evil spirits were prominent in idolatrous worship, God commanded them not to be contaminated with such worship. All occult practices are very definitely forbidden by God, and are the sole work of the devil, and as such they are condemned by Scripture: "Let no-one be found among you who sacrifices his son or daughter in the fire, who practises divination or sorcery, interprets omens, engages in witchcraft, or casts spells, or who is a medium or spiritist or who consults the dead. Anyone who does these things is detestable to the Lord" (Dt 18:10–12). Again, in Leviticus 19:31, "Do not turn to mediums or seek out spiritists, for you will be defiled by them. I am the Lord your God."

As we have seen in the previous chapters, the devil

had many who worshipped him in the form of false gods, and he works in the same way today. Until the middle of our century, witchcraft and devil worship seemed to have taken a back seat. Although it was still going on behind the scenes, more attention and interest was given to new scientific discoveries. In 1951 however, the English courts repealed the country's witchcraft act, a law almost forgotten since 1735. Although to most people this seemed insignificant, it proved a major breakthrough to those who practised witchcraft. What had previously been done in secret now became more open, apart from the activities of the black witches, who for the most part prefer to remain secret.

There are many thousands involved in some form of occultism. In 1980 there were an estimated twenty million people in Europe alone. Judging from the increased interest in these things, the number may well have doubled by now.

In my first book *From Witchcraft to Christ* (Concordia 1973), I described much of what went on in the satanist temples, but much was omitted, which I now feel should be exposed. The temples of Satan were mostly situated in large houses which belonged to the richer members of the movement. Walls were torn down inside the houses to provide space for at least 400 worshippers. The temples were never left unattended; some satanists were always in residence to guard the temple from outsiders, and to care for the upkeep of the temple and its contents.

The walls were covered with effigies of Satan, half man, half beast, with cloven hoofs and horns, protruding tongue and ears. Satan can take on any form satanists wish. There are no seats for worshippers. Satanists were there an hour before any ceremony began, no-one was late. If you were late and did not give a very good reason, you were punished by whipping. When you worshipped the devil you stood for hours with arms upraised, or you prostrated yourself on the floor, which was usually made of marble, and engraved with snakes, dragons and flames of fire. On the high altar were cups, knives, bowls, snuffers and candlesticks all made from solid gold and silver. At the side of the altar was a throne-like seat, where the chief satanist sat. The throne itself was carved with expert skill and cunning, with snakes, dragons and flames of fire. The chief satanist's robes were made from the very best black velvet, and embroidered in gold threads with the same snakes, dragons and flames. All this work must have taken a great deal of time and money, but satanists spare no time or expense. There is nothing cheap or imitative in the satanist temples, but in fact, it is all an imitation of what God has. Take the satanist bible for instance. Because God has a book, the Bible, the devil has to have one. They call it the satanist's bible; I prefer to call it an evil book. It is a very poor imitation indeed, since it is filled with evil revelations from former chief priests, which date back over centuries. Here again, no expense was spared for the upkeep of these ancient manuscripts; each one was beautifully bound with gold. No-one could remove them from the temples, except for the chief satanist. Their main teaching, regarding the origin and fall of Satan, has already been described. They also teach that black is white and white is black; that good is evil and evil is good; and that light is darkness and darkness light. Everything is twisted round the opposite way. No matter how stupid this teaching sounds, many believe it; I did once. When you are repeatedly told the same thing, over and over again, you begin to believe it; it is just like a massive brain-washing. We get a very clear picture of witchcraft and satanism from Isaiah 5:20: ''Woe to those who call evil good and good evil, who put darkness for light and light for darkness, who put bitter for sweet and sweet for bitter.'' When I first saw this in the Bible, I was surprised, and showed it to other Christians who were most enlightened by it; it exposes witchcraft and satanism very well indeed.

The satanist book is six times thicker than the average Bible, yet I was able to learn it by heart in a very short time. I did not understand this fully myself at the time, but now I realise how I did it—Satan educated me. Satan does not care two hoots what kind of educational background you have. You can be as thick as two planks, he does not worry about that; all he asks, demands in fact, is allegiance to him and his cause. He will do the rest. When I left school at the age of fourteen, I could barely read and write, yet when I became a prostitute, drug addict and witch, I learned very quickly the ways of evil. When I became queen of black witches and travelled to France, Holland, Germany and South Africa, I was able to converse with people, and teach them the evil art of witchcraft, having never learned their languages. This was a surprise even to the chief satanist, who was unable to achieve this himself.

Satan is educating people today. How do very young children pick up so quickly the bad things, while they are often slow in picking up that which is right and good? Satan is poisoning young minds today by many different means. Video nasties are one of them, depicting dreadful acts of violence, murder, rape, pornography, horror and the occult. Although there has been a clampdown on video nasties, they are still around. Filthy magazines are still being published and sold, and some are on open display for all to see. Sex shops are still open to the public, and some of these sell books on the occult. There are magazines which publish advertisements inviting inquiries about the occult world, and many are falling into the evil web of witchcraft. It is all part of the devil's educational and recruitment programme. I thank my lovely Saviour that when I received him into my life, He uneducated me, and then he re-educated me in the things of God.

People are ignorant of the dangers of even the slightest involvement in occult practices. Little did I realise what I was getting bound up with when I first got involved. No-one warned me of the dangers, because no-one knew about it but the satanists themselves, and they were not going to warn me of what to expect. It is far easier to get into however, than to get out of, as I and others later found out. This is the very reason why I warn people, and expose the occult, no matter what form it takes, and tell them the way out of it all. There is only one way out, and that is through the salvation and deliverance of Christ, who said, ''I am the way and the truth and the life'' (Jn 14:6).

I have actually burned Bibles and other Christian books in satanist temples; it is all part of the ceremony in every temple. In each temple there are two huge torches crossing each other at either side of the high altar which, when lit, provide light for the temple and fire on which Christian books are burned. I have held Bible after Bible for a full half hour in the white hot flames, until they have disintegrated in ashes, and my hands have remained unburned. This shows how real Satan is, but it proves a far more important point than that—it proves how much Satan hates and fears the word of God, and anything Christian. All the more reason then, for Christians to read and study God's word, and believe God's word, and act upon it. God's word can put the devil to flight. The Bible I once hated and despised, burned and ridiculed, I now love with all my heart, and believe that it is the sole and infallible word of God, inspired by the Holy Spirit from cover to cover. It is our only safeguard from evil and deceit: it is full of God's promises, which never fail; it is a source of inspiration, encouragement and blessing.

One young satanist I know actually gave her whole hand to Satan as a sacrifice in the satanist temple. They took one of the swords from the high altar, kissed it, and raised it high in the air, then cut off her hand and offered it to the devil on a silver platter. Everyone was in a trance-like state, and thought it was a wonderful miracle, because the girl felt no pain. Her arm was then cauterised in the flames of the torch. That girl, and others who at various times gave fingers and toes to the devil, were maimed for life—and what for? Absolutely nothing! What did Satan do for them? Nothing but bring them misery and pain! Jesus said this of the devil and how true it is, ''The thief comes only to steal and kill and destroy.'' Thank God He went on to say, ''I have come that they may have life, and have it to the full" (Jn 10:10). I am so glad that I did not sacrifice any part of my body to Satan. I believe that the Lord kept me from that, because He knew that one day He would save me, deliver me from the power of the devil, and use me for His glory, to lead others to Himself and warn of the terrible dangers and the evil of occult practices.

Satan desired a throne while he was in heaven, God's throne, but what he could not get while he was in heaven, he gets right down here on earth. Although the devil has set up many elaborate thrones and altars on the earth in temples of Satan and witches' covens, the greatest throne he has is the throne-room of men's and women's hearts. He sits on the throne of their hearts and minds, ruling over them and influencing human decisions over the affairs of nations. He is "the ruler of the kingdom of the air, the spirit who is now at work in those who are disobedient" (Eph 2:2).

Satan knows full well that he cannot possibly persuade everyone to worship him directly in satanist temples or witches' covens, so he blinds people's minds to the truth some other way, and gets the same result: a denial of God. He tells people that there is no heaven and no hell, no God and no devil. He tells thousands that there is no life beyond the grave, and that the Bible is just an old-fashioned book, written by old-fashioned superstitious men; OK for small children maybe, but not for grown-up educated men and women. Satan is the god of this world: "The god of this age has blinded the minds of unbelievers, so that they cannot see the light of the gospel of the glory of Christ, who is the image of God" (2 Co 4:4). The world loves pleasures and riches more than God. Jesus said this in John 3:19–20: "This is the verdict: Light has come into the world, but men loved darkness instead of light because their deeds were evil. Everyone who does evil hates the light, and will not come into the light for fear that his deeds will be exposed." Some people do not realise just how dark some darkness is, and this can certainly be said of those who are caught in the trap of occultism.

In Revelation 3:9 we read of those who say they are Jews but are of "the synagogue of Satan." This is so very true of all those who practise witchcraft and satanism. Their evil temples are indeed sanctuaries of Satan, the synagogues of Satan. In my first book, *From Witchcraft to Christ*, I described the difference between witches' covens and satanists' temples, but for the benefit of those who still do not know, it is worth repeating. Satanists need a temple and always worship the devil through the chief satanist or a high priest or priestess. Different orders have slightly different rules. Witches, black and white, always gather together in covens, made up of thirteen people, six male and six female if possible, and one being the head, who is called the high priest or priestess. They need no temple; they worship anywhere they can but prefer a secluded place such as a clearing in the woods or a lonely beach, or if indoors, again they prefer a place that is isolated. Their numbers are smaller, but only when they are counted in groups or covens. Altogether the numbers go into many thousands, all over the world.

In God's sight there is absolutely no difference between black and white witchcraft; it is all evil and forbidden by God in Scripture. Because of confusion in people's minds regarding white and black witchcraft, some people think that white witchcraft is all right because they claim they do no harm. This is a gross lie; white witches do a lot of harm. Their religion is as pagan as black witchcraft, their god is Mother Earth, and they call upon and believe in mythological spirits and gods. They chant and dance in their ceremonies, and their sexual rites are disgusting, to say the least. They claim they do no harm yet they do not hesitate to put curses on those who are their enemies, using voodoo methods to do so. They claim they bring rain for the farmers, find lost objects or lost loved ones, heal people and charge no fee for doing it. This is again a total lie. They manage to extract huge sums of money for their favours, by deceiving people with smooth talk. The increased interest in witchcraft is alarming, but it proves the fact that Satan is waging an all-out war against the church of God. God's people are going to come into contact with it one way or another, so it is wise to know just what we are up against.

Jesus spoke of the things that would happen upon the earth in the last days: ''And many false prophets will appear and deceive many people. Because of the increase of wickedness, the love of most will grow cold'' (Mt 24:11–12). Again in verse 24: ''For false Christs and false prophets will appear and perform great signs and miracles to deceive even the elect.'' Christians should not be afraid about these things, but should instead rejoice, for the coming of the Lord draws near. If we are ignorant and fearful, we cannot fight the good fight of faith with full assurance of victory. Those who are members of the family of God need not fear the evil one, and no witch's curse can affect the child of God. We are instructed in God's word to be alert and watchful and to be clad in the armour which God supplies through His eternal Son. With Christ as our Captain we can face the evil one and his dark angels day by day, hour by hour, fearlessly, knowing that He goes before us. As we abide in Christ, and Christ abides in us, and as we claim His promises in prayer, we stand invincible.

Another sanctuary of Satan is the spiritist movement. One baneful symptom of today's spiritual warfare is a recrudescence of spiritism, the attempt to hold communication with the spirits of the dead through the agency of mediums. The revival of spiritism should not surprise or alarm us as we heed the prophecy of Paul, ''The Spirit clearly says that in later times some will abandon the faith and follow deceiving spirits and things taught by demons'' (1 Ti 4:1).

There are many who delight in dabbling in the mysterious, and the occult offers something spooky, which has the attraction of a candle for the moth. The movement has gained its greatest numbers from among the bereaved, who are seeking comfort and consolation regarding their lost loved ones. Our sympathy goes out to them, but the tragedy is when the bereaved resort to what is forbidden by God. The church is partly to blame for not sounding a clear warning note, and for not providing healing and comfort for a sufficient length of time after bereavement.

Two of the early founders of the movement were Margaret and Kate Fox. Both died from alcoholism, but not before they had both openly renounced the spiritist cult. In 1888 Margaret Fox said in front of her sister, "I am here tonight as one of the founders of spiritism, to denounce it as absolute falsehood, the most wicked blasphemy the world has ever known." If ever the devil manifests himself as "an angel of light" it is at the spiritist seance. Christ spoke an eternal truth when He said "By their fruit you will recognise them" (Mt 7:20). Judged by its fruit, spiritism has very little to offer the seeker. On the contrary, the effects of spiritism on those who have been involved has been disastrous. The physical effects on the mediums is startling and frightening. They frequently fall to the floor, roll around, and have been known to froth at the mouth; just as those who were demon-possessed in Christ's day. Often they go into spasms but this is supposed to be OK because they are "getting through" to the spirit world; which is quite true, they are getting through to the spirit world, but what they do not know or accept, is that they are getting through to evil spirits. They of course think they are getting through to good spirits or departed spirits. There is only one good Spirit, and that is the Holy Spirit, which comes from God. Their workers are often rendered more and more nervous, more and more excitable, and many have gone completely insane. The effects on the ignorant followers is worse still; many thousands have been confined to mental hospitals through having tampered with the supernatural. Is this the mark of spirituality, the possession of "a sound mind"? (2 Ti 1:7 AV).

A passage of Scripture that forms part of the foundation of the spiritist movement is 1 Samuel 28, but wrongly interpreted, this incident becomes a liability rather than an asset. The passage records a solitary instance in which someone who had died reappeared. Disregarding the explicit command of God, Saul resorted to the witch of Endor for comfort, for he was now out of touch with God. He asked for Samuel to be brought up. To the utter astonishment of both Saul and the medium, God interrupted the seance by causing Samuel himself to appear. Note that in this scriptural record it plainly states, "Samuel said to Saul," (verse 15) thus ruling out any possibility of an impersonating evil spirit. It would seem that God (who had every right to do so) allowed Samuel to appear in order to deliver to Saul the last terrible message of God's rejection.

It is clear from the scriptural record that Samuel did not appear at the call of the witch, or else why should she be so astonished, and cry out with a loud voice? In any case, this solitary instance would be slender evidence on which to base the whole supernatural structure of the spiritist system.

The main reason for rejecting the spiritist movement is its attitude to the written word of God. They have said themselves, "To assert that it is a holy and divine book, that God inspired the writers to make known the will of God, is a gross outrage, and misleading to the public" (*Cults and Isms*, J. O. Saunders, Lakeland (1984) p. 13). "The miraculous conception of Christ is merely a fabulous tale" (*Spiritual Telegraph*, number 37). "Advanced spirits do not teach the atonement of Christ. It is an absurd idea that Jesus was more divine that any other man. Christ was a medium and a reformer in Judea. He is now an advanced spirit in the sixth sphere. Tom Paine is in the seventh sphere, one above the Lord" (Dr Weisse, noted spiritist). "Man is his own saviour" (Rev. W. Stainton Moses).

It would be strange indeed, if God left us with no infallible test of the nature of this pseudo-religion. "Do not believe every spirit, but test the spirits to see whether they are from God." How do we test them? Do they speak according to, and in harmony with the word of God? To ask this question is to answer it. Do they confess that Jesus Christ is come in the flesh? If they do not, they are not of God, but are the spirit of the anti-christ (1 Jn 4:1–3).

I think I have given sufficient evidence to make anyone seeking after truth shun any connection with spiritism, whatever form it takes. To those who are already ensnared by it, God's word is "Come out from among them and be separate . . . touch no unclean thing" (2 Co 6:17).

It is absolutely amazing to me how many people are so gullible, and take for granted what is told them without first testing it, and proving it to be of God. Multitudes eagerly accept teachings that leave them at liberty to please themselves, and obey the promptings of the carnal mind. Satan beguiles people now, as he beguiled Eve in the Garden of Eden, by flattery, and by kindling a desire to obtain knowledge by encouraging ambition for self-exaltation. We read in Isaiah 8:19: "When men tell you to consult mediums and spiritists, who whisper and mutter, should not a people enquire of their God?" If only men and women sought the Lord on every point of their lives, and did not stray from the word of God, He would show them the pathway, and He alone would guide them into all truth. Thousands reject the word of God as unworthy of belief, but in eager confidence accept the deceptions of Satan. Satan has been long preparing for his final effort to deceive the world. The foundation of his work was laid by the false assurance given to Eve in the Garden of Eden "you will not surely die . . . For God knows that when you eat of it your eyes will be opened, and you will be like God, knowing good and evil" (Ge 3:4). People think they are going to live and die knowing all things, and some live as if they are never going to die at all.

Little by little, Satan has prepared the way for his masterpiece of deception in the development of the occult in its various forms. He has not yet reached the full accomplishment of his designs, but they will be reached in the last remnant of time. We read in Revelation 16:13–14, ''Then I saw three evil spirits that looked like frogs; they came out of the mouth of the dragon, out of the mouth of the beast and out of the mouth of the false prophet. They are spirits of demons performing miraculous signs, and they go out to the kings of the whole world, to gather them for the battle on the great day of God Almighty.'' Except for those who are kept by the power of God, through faith in his word, the whole world would be swept into the ranks of this delusion. People are fast being lulled into a sense of false security, to be awakened only by the outpouring of the wrath of God.

It is imperative that soldiers of Christ stand up and be counted. We are needed more than ever before to fight the good fight of faith, to spread the good news of salvation to the lost, to warn, rebuke and shun evil. Be assured that God is stronger than His foes. The wicked one cannot break through the guard which God has stationed about His people. There is no limit to the power and authority Christ has given to those who watch and wait for his appearing.

There are a great many more evil places that can be classed as ''the sanctuaries of Satan'' like the cinema clubs that show x-rated films, strip clubs, and other clubs, some of which are for members only, not to mention the secret society of the ''freemasons'' whose activities are as devilish as any witchcraft coven. Whenever there is a club whose activities are questionable, and secret, you can be sure that the adversary is behind it. Many of our young people, who have left school, and are unable to find employment often set up their own clubs to keep themselves amused, as they cannot afford to pay to get into the expensive clubs and entertainment centres, and who knows what they get up to? Gangs of young people, with nothing to do, and nowhere to go, who roam our streets at night, are easy pickings for evil men and women, who lure them away with promises of fame and easy money, and often they end up on the streets as prostitutes, and involved in other evil activities.

The devil roams around like a roaring lion, looking for those he can devour. It is up to us to warn them, and point them to the Saviour, who alone is able to break the bondage of sin and darkness that fills their hearts and lives. We as Christians can break down the strongholds of Satan. With Christ as our leader, our Captain, and our King, there is *nothing* we cannot do, for we know that our Jesus will go before us. He will prepare the way for us to reach out to those who are bound in spiritual darkness, in ''the synagogues of Satan'' and bring them into the light.

CHAPTER NINE

Signposts to Jesus' coming

JESUS was asked by His disciples what would be the sign of His coming, and the sign of the end of the age. Jesus gave them His reply in the form of a parable; the parable of the fig-tree sprouting the first leaves to indicate the nearness of the Summer (Mt 24:32–35). An accumulation of events on the earth and in the sky, would signal the arrival of God's judgments upon those who would witness these things, yet take no notice.

The events which would accumulate are plainly described in Matthew 24, "Many will come in my name claiming, 'I am the Christ,' and will deceive many" (verse 5). Many have already been deceived in the past by claiming that they were the Christ: many are still being deceived today by false prophets bringing false doctrines, false security, and false peace. The devil, as I have mentioned before, is the arch deceiver, the greatest deceiver of all time.

"You will hear of wars and rumours of wars" (verse 6). War is being waged in Northern Ireland and in the Middle East, for despite the fact that the Gulf War has been declared over, war is still being waged there; the Kurdish people are still suffering untold misery and pain. The war is not over for them. Many thousands have died and been injured and maimed in what is regarded in some places as a holy war. Nothing could be further from the truth. The devil is the author of wars and bloodshed, and he has stretched his bloody hand and stained the heart of our own nation. "Nation will rise against nation, and kingdom against kingdom" (verse 7). There is much unrest, suspicion and distrust among nations today; the fear of the atom bomb is real. Men have the capability of wiping out complete nations with the press of a button.

"Many will turn away from the faith and will betray and hate each other" (verse 10). The devil is using his own devices to blame God; he is using trials, pain, sorrow, persecution, fear and disappointments as tools to turn men and women away from God. "Because of the increase of wickedness, the love of most will grow cold" (verse 12). Because of these things, people, even Christians, have become cold and indifferent towards the things of God.

To further illustrate His coming, Christ gave an historical allegory about the great flood in the days of Noah (verses 36–39). He said that people were going about their business as usual—eating and drinking, marrying and giving in marriage, but paid no attention to the warnings of Noah about impending judgment. Their ears were deafened and their eyes were blinded to the truth by Satan, and they had no idea that God's prophetic time of judgment had come until the flood came and destroyed them all.

We are told that the coming of Christ will be similar to the destruction of Sodom. Two angels told Lot that God was going to punish the wicked residents of that city, and they escorted Lot and his family to safety. The people of Sodom went about their daily business, eating and drinking, buying and selling, planting and building, but the day Lot left that city God rained down fire and brimstone, and Sodom was destroyed (Lk 17: 28–29). Jesus said that His coming would be exactly like that. There is a pattern! First there is a prophetic warning, then God removes His people, and then lastly judgment falls upon the unbelievers.

The days immediately prior to this will reveal to the world Satan's capacity for evil, but they will even more reveal the triumphant power of God. *There will exist side by side, a steadfast faith in some, and spiritual apostasy in others*—a situation clearly foretold in the Scriptures. Peter, on the day of Pentecost, spoke of a last-day outpouring of the Holy Spirit (Ac 2:17). Paul on the other hand, wrote about a latter-day departure from the faith (1 Ti 4:1). It has been the spiritual outpouring that has induced the counteracting surge of iniquity. Now it has become necessary for the Holy Spirit to restrain the works of Satan, for it is only the power of the Holy Spirit that can check the power of evil in the last days. Except for the presence of the Holy Spirit, this world today would be overrun with evil people like Idi Amin, Father Divine, Hitler, Stalin, Saddam Hussein, and worse. Much worse! Worse men than these shall soon rise up, as part of an attempted takeover by the anti-Christian influences. Iniquity and spiritual deception would be unchecked were it not for the restraining power of the Holy Spirit.

The Scriptures teach us that men and women must repent and turn to God so that their sins may be blotted out, and that times of refreshing may come from the Lord, and that he may send the Christ who must remain in heaven until the time comes for God to restore everything, as promised long ago through the prophets (Ac 3:19–21). That time has almost come! God's word is basically a book of restoration. After the fall of man into sin in the Garden of Eden, God promised to restore to man fellowship with Himself. The succeeding generations of mankind were alienated from God because of imputed sin. They too were in need of restoration. The process God chose to bring this about was that of redemption through the shed blood of His Son, Jesus Christ.

The final instrument for the accomplishment of God's purposes of restoration, is the church. Yet the New Testament church failed and lapsed into the dark ages. The church itself needed to be restored to its former glory, so that He might accomplish the ultimate restoration of believers to perfection. The New Testament Greek word for restoration is *apokatastasis*. It means to set something back into its former state.

Through the restored church the gospel, in all its fullness, is being preached all over the world. Jesus Himself said this would happen before he came back; "And this gospel of the kingdom will be preached in the whole world as a testimony to all nations, and then the end will come" (Mt 24:14).

During the dark ages the church declined and lost its strength. Who, and what, caused that decline? No-one but Satan himself. It is the devil that causes the church of God to grow cold and indifferent towards the things of God. The arch-enemy of souls robbed the church of the truth: the truth of salvation through faith (Ac 16:30–31); of water baptism by immersion (Ac 8:38–39); the truth regarding holiness and sanctification (2 Co 6:17, 7:1); the truth regarding healing which was practised by the early church (Ac 5:16, Mk 16:18); the truth regarding praise and worship (Ac 16:25); the truth of laying on of hands and prophecy (Ac 13:3, 1 Ti 4:14); and the truth of the baptism of the Holy Spirit (Ac 2:1–6).

The early believers submitted to the Lordship of Christ (Ac 2:36–40) and led lives of holiness (Ac 6:3, 11:24, 20:32). They were led by the Spirit (Ac 11:12). They had great joy (Ac 13:52). They experienced supernatural signs and wonders (Ac 2:43, 5:12, 8:13). There was church growth (Ac 2:41). There was long-suffering in times of persecution (Ac 4:1–41, 5:17–42). There was edification of one another (Ac 9:31). The word of God was spread (Ac 6:7). They were founded on the word of God (Ac 1:15–20). They had spiritual authority over evil powers (Ac 8:7, 16:16–18).

What happened to this triumphant church? As Christianity spread throughout the known world, there evolved a gradual mix with the practice of pagan religions. Impurity and compromise with worldly views began to be tolerated. Total commitment to the local church was no longer emphasised. False teaching crept into the church, bringing decline, spiritual blindness, loss of vision and loss of power. The New Testament prophets confirm this. They said it would happen (2 Pe 2:1–3, Ac 20:28–31). False ministries went unhindered (2 Pe 2:1–9). There was loss of spiritual hunger for the truth (1 Ti 4:1–2). There were self-willed believers (2 Pe 2:10). There was carnal indulgence (Eph 2:3). There was spiritual lukewarmness (Rev 3:15–16). There was worldliness (1 Jn 2:15–17). There was loss of vision (2 Pe 1:9, 1 Jn 2:11). The early church witnessed the apostolic ministry, but after the death of the last apostle John, the apostolic ministry disappeared. There was no evidence of the apostolic ministry continuing after John.

In 140 AD, the ministry of the prophet vanished. In 150 AD, the gifts of the Holy Spirit began to disappear. Bit by bit the church was stripped of its truths, its strength, its power, its glory, its vision.

In 225 AD, church membership became a matter of agreeing with a creed, and was no longer based on conversion.

By 240 AD, holiness had disappeared as worldliness infiltrated the church. The church continued its decline, reaching its lowest ebb in the dark ages.

God has been restoring truth in the same order as it was lost. In 1517, God began to restore the most fundamental of all doctrines—justification by faith. Martin Luther was used by God in restoring this doctrine as opposed to a system of justification by works.

In the seventeenth century, a dynamic spiritual life with Christ, based upon correctness of life as well as doctrine, began to be restored.

In 1750, sanctification and holiness began to be restored to the church under the ministry of John Wesley.

In 1900, the baptism in the Holy Spirit began to be restored to the church, under the ministry of A. B. Simpson, and others.

In 1906, the gifts of the Holy Spirit, and the five-fold ministry of Ephesians 4:4–11 began to be restored in the Azusa revival.

In 1948, the doctrine of laying on of hands of the Presbytery began to be restored and spontaneous praise and worship was restored, with the singing of spiritual songs, in the Canadian revival.

Today there is a great movement of God among His people. What the devil robbed the church of, is being restored. There is a great spiritual awakening in our churches. The devil does not like it one bit, and he is fighting to keep the church of God bound, blind, cold and indifferent. There are still those who will not respond to what the Lord is doing, and are content to stay where they are. We should learn an important lesson. God is still moving His people on, and we must be willing and ready to move forward with Him.

The restoration of the church to its former glory, power and strength, with joy and praise, vision and faith, victory over evil, holiness and truth, is one of the major signposts pointing to the near return of Christ for His radiant, spotless church. Elijah prepared the way for Elisha. John the Baptist prepared the way for the Lord. The Lord prepared the way for the church. The restored church is preparing the way for the second coming of Christ for His bride, the church.

We are rapidly approaching the time when God's day of grace will cease and Christ will return to snatch away His waiting bride (the true church)—those who are waiting and watching for His coming. The warning sound is being heard again as Christ's near return is being heralded in the four corners of this globe. There can be no excuse from the people of the earth that no warning was given to them. The people of God need not fear the fast-moving events leading up to the return of Christ. Their tremendous significance should gladden the heart of every believer, for the coming of the Lord draws nearer and nearer, the time when the dead in Christ will be raised, and those who are alive and remain will be caught up to meet Him in the air (1 Th 4:16–17).

Let us take a look at some of the other major signposts pointing to the coming of Christ. One is the return of the dispersed Jews to become a nation again in 1948, and the Jews recapture of the Old City of Jerusalem in the 1967 Arab-Israeli War. In spite of 2000 years of being scattered, the Jewish people have preserved a distinct national identity. During all the years of dispersion, these people have suffered the most cruel persecution ever endured by any other nation of people, and yet, Jewish history with all its tragedies and triumphs has been foretold in the Bible. Moses predicted they would be chastened or disciplined for not believing their God, and rejecting his ways. Moses predicted that a mighty nation would invade and destroy Israel and the prophet Isaiah added details to his prophetic warning about 150 years before it occurred: ''The time will surely come when everything in your palace, and all that your fathers have stored up until this day, will be carried off to Babylon. Nothing will be left, says the Lord'' (Isa 39:6). It all happened exactly as it was predicted. The Babylonians swept into the Southern kingdom of Israel and Jerusalem and it was destroyed. Moses, who predicted the first stage of discipline, also predicted the second stage. As the time of enslavement (which was 70 years) came to an end, the Persian king Cyrus released some of the Jews who had survived the horror and destruction to return and rebuild the temple in Jerusalem, and yet they continued in their disbelief and rejection of God.

Moses said that Israel would once again be destroyed as a nation. The survivors would then be scattered throughout the world in every nation. In Deuteronomy 28:64–68, Moses gave a clear and accurate description of what it would be like: ''Then the Lord will scatter you among all nations, from one end of the earth to the other . . . There the Lord will give you an anxious mind, eyes weary with longing, and a despairing heart. You will live in constant suspense, filled with dread both night and day, never sure of your life . . . There you will offer yourselves for sale to your enemies as male and female slaves, but no-one will buy you.'' Other prophets like Isaiah, Jeremiah, Ezekiel and Amos, foretold the worldwide exile of the Jewish nation and its destruction. Jesus said it would happen, and used

these words: ''When you see Jerusalem being surrounded by armies, you will know that its desolation is
near'' (Lk 21: 20). He said they would ''fall by the sword
and will be taken as prisoners to all the nations. Jerusalem will be trampled on by the Gentiles until the
times of the Gentiles are fulfilled'' (Lk 21:24). It all happened! Less than forty years after the death of Christ,
Titus and the Roman armies destroyed Jerusalem,
slaying thousands. Those who survived were shipped
off to the slave markets of Egypt. For almost 2000 years
the Jews wandered around the earth with no country of
their own, in constant fear of their lives. Christians have
watched in utter amazement and compassion, as the
suffering of the Jewish nation became a worldwide
phenomenon. Israel's history of heartache, misery, sorrow and pain, exactly matched and fulfilled prophetic
warnings from God, which should teach us all a lesson:
when God says He will do something, He will do it.
God means what He says.

The same prophets who foretold the massive exile of
the Jews, also foretold their final restoration as a nation
before countdown to the coming of Christ to this world.
Many things have happened since the recapture of the
old city of Jersualem in 1967. We heard how thousands
of Ethiopian Jews were airlifted from their famine-
stricken land to Israel. The secret airlift of thousands of
starving people required superb efficiency, the exact
details of this rescue were a closely guarded secret. The
Ethiopians stumbled barefoot from the planes clutching
cans of water, because they believed Israel had no
water. Some kissed the ground and asked, ''Are we
really in Zion?'' That flight into the twentieth century
must have been a frightening experience for the
thousands of bewildered black Jews who had never
been inside a plane before. The Israeli government, despite their own problems of growing unemployment,
put these Ethiopians before any other consideration. It
was a leap forward for the Ethiopian Jews, it was also a
leap forward in the fulfilment of Biblical prophecy.
Every month more and more Jews are returning to

Israel, and no opposition will stop the Jews returning to their homeland. *The stage has been set, the players are in place, and no-one can stop the great plan of God. The devil cannot stop the plan of God.* Not only has the actual State of Israel been restored, through the efforts of the Jews, but spiritual Israel is being restored; the true church of Jesus Christ. Jesus is building His church, and the gates of hell shall not prevail against it (Mt 16:18).

The devil does not like it when Biblical prophecy is being fulfilled, because he knows it signifies the beginning of the end for him, and he knows that there is absolutely nothing he can do about it. As might be expected, the mightiest of recorders, Martin Luther, seems to have been a special target of the devil. Luther's biographers made much of his conflicts with Satan. These included a story that once, while translating the New Testament in Warburg Castle, he became so aware of the presence of the devil that he threw an inkwell at the apparition. In his excellent biography *Luther* Rudolf Thiel says that the devil attacked Luther with his utmost power and craftiness and thought to bring him down. Much earlier, Thomas Carlyle recorded that Luther on one occasion wrote, ''I have seen and defied innumerable devils.'' The devil always attacks the truth of Christ's return, so much so that even those who say they are Christians are ignoring the signs of the times recorded in Scripture.

The rapid decline of sexual morality is another sign of the times we are living in today. The devil is twisting the real meaning of love into something ugly, mean and hurtful. The divorce rate has shot up alarmingly, and it is now easier to get a divorce. Abortion and VD rates have soared. Illegitimacy has risen, despite contraception, so much so in fact, that in the past fifteen years legitimate births have only risen by twenty per cent compared to illegitimate births which have risen by a hundred per cent.

The Bible tells us that God is love, and shows us what His love is like. ''But God demonstrates his own love for us in this: While we were still sinners, Christ died for us'' (Ro 5:8). And again in John 3:16, ''For God so loved the world that he gave his one and only Son, that whoever believes in him shall not perish but have eternal life.'' God's love is unselfish. In the name of so-called love today (what some people call ''free love''), many a heart and home has been broken and darkened. There is much that passes for real love, but in fact it is just lust masquerading as love. For lust says, ''I want, so I must have,'' while real love says, ''I must give.'' God is not against real love. Real love is a pure and wonderful gift from God. It is the devil who has tainted human love, for it is often mixed with jealousy and vanity, and it can be selfish and thoughtless. The Bible tells us that ''God is love.'' It does not say, ''As long as love is present, love rules, and you can do as you please.'' God's love never degrades, it is not selfish; the love which God gives is personal, and lasting, satisfying and ennobling and sacrificial. Does God's love stop? Of course not! But affairs do. There is much talk about endless devotion and self-sacrifice, but afterwards all that is left is a tangled web of disillusionment, depression, self reproach, and broken empty hearts. The devil tells many that this kind of love will last forever, but all it brings is loneliness, fear and guilt. Does real love hurt? If you really love someone, would you expose them to hurt and pain? Yet there is plenty of hurt and pain where sex outside of marriage is concerned. There is plenty of pain when adultery is committed. What about abortion? Who gets hurt then? The young woman herself, her family, and everyone concerned. The devil is behind the collapse of families; it is him who is the author of misery, depriving parents of children, and children of parents, he is robbing children of love and protection, joy and happiness, and warmth and security.

The Bible tells us that, ''Perfect love casteth out fear'' (1 Jn 4:18 AV) and this is true. For those who know Him and trust Him, God gives peace of mind and binds up the wounds that transgression has made. The same

Bible passage states that "fear hath torment." Think of the torment of a young woman who fears that she is doing wrong, but cannot get out of the situation she finds herself in: the torment that she may be pregnant; the fear of her parents finding out that she is having an affair with a married man, and the fear that the relationship will not last.

What about homosexuality which is rampant today? Who hurts? Who fears? Who feels trapped? What about the misery, shame and guilt this brings? Does love do that? No, but the devil does! The evil part about it all, is that it is accepted by society as normal. Smutty jokes are made all the time about homosexuality, and many are afraid to use the word *gay* because of its association. It has now become a dirty word.

Who gets hurt when rape is committed? Everyone involved! Many of our lovely young women have been scarred for life in their minds; others face a long hard journey back to self-respect, although the offence was not their fault. Rape today is not confined to the dark streets, homes are being broken into and often violence is used to a terrible degree. It has become unsafe to walk the streets after dark for fear of being raped, mugged, or both. No, it's not just the dark streets, it's the light streets as well; it's done in the daytime. It is frightening, but it's true, and the devil, the one who manages to convince people he does not exist, is behind every dark and evil deed.

Lies and deceit accompany promiscuous sex, and who is the author of lies and deceit? No-one else but the devil who is the father of lies. All lovers think their love will last forever, but it does not always turn out that way—hearts get broken. It's a horrible thing to be jilted. It brings a fear of trusting people, even those you love. Real love is very challenging in a wonderful way. Love does not go around demanding responses, that is why real love is so liberating. It's a wonderful thing to be able to trust someone and to know you are trusted in return. At one time you could trust people's word, but today being let down is an everyday occurrence. That old saying that, ''a gentleman's word is his bond,'' seems almost obsolete, and sad to say, even Christians break their word and let people down. Many today have trusted someone entirely, only to be let down badly and as a result of which they find it very hard to trust again.

In this world there are many who are not accepted by society. They are in fact, rejects, cast aside by those who are considered to be more attractive or intelligent. These are the ones who are the most gullible and grasp at anything that looks like love, only to find out that it was false and unreal. God's love is a faithful love, He never lets anyone down, He is faithful and true, and His love never ends.

God loves us, not because we are lovable, but because of His grace; not because we deserve it, but because He is love. His name is love. God's love accepts us just as we are, crooked nose, warts and all. God's love challenges us to love the unloveable, to love our enemies, and those who have treated us wrongly. God, because He loves us, does not cover up our sins and pretend they are not there. God's love shows up our failures, and shortcomings. He wants us to see sin for what it is. He came to die for our sins, in the person of His Son, Jesus Christ. Jesus gave His life so that our sins can be forgiven, and to barricade the way to hell. God's love is honest. The devil's work today is to blind people to the pure, unfailing love of God, to deceive them about real love and what it really means, and to give them a false love. This should challenge us to reflect the love of God wherever we go, and talk to people about the love of God.

There is widespread drug addiction today. It's now easier to obtain drugs than ever before, and young people everywhere are in danger from the dealers in drugs. The authorities are more and more concerned; there has been much talk, and much written about drugs and the damage they cause, but still drug addiction is increasing at an alarming rate. Drug addiction is a kind of chemical enslavement—and who is the

113

enslaver? The devil, the enemy of souls, and the hardest task-master ever known. That old saying, "the devil looks after his own," is complete nonsense, and a gross lie. When the devil has finished with you, he throws you on the rubbish dump and makes you into a reject. The devil tells the vulnerable, the lonely, the depressed, and those with deep-rooted problems, that drugs will not harm them if they just take a little now and then to ease the tension. A baby rattlesnake has just as much poison as a fully grown one and just as much venom—just enough to kill. Many start out by experimenting with so-called soft drugs, and end up as hopeless hard drug addicts.

Addiction brings out all the worst characteristics of a personality, and due to the progression of psychological and spiritual decay, it becomes increasingly difficult for a non-addict to form a relationship with the addict, who then feels more and more of an outcast. Education and prevention are important in the battle against drug addiction and alcoholism. These are two conditions with similar causes, and in many respects, similar results.

But these measures of prevention are not sufficient if we have nothing to offer in return to fill the void and the emptiness of life, and remedy the insecurity which crushes the personality of the addict. The way Christ offers is not easy—in fact, initially, it may appear much harder than the quick answer of a bottle, a pill, or a needle. The devil will make it look harder than it really is for the hopeless addict. This is another one of the clever tricks of Satan. He will try and make them give up, before they even get started.

There is one ray of light in the seemingly hopeless plight of the addict. Christians are no longer afraid of addicts, and are reaching out to them. There are now centres opening up for those caught in the web of drugs, if they are willing to be helped. They can receive understanding, counsel and guidance, and some are being set free from the awful bondage of drugs. The devil is not having all his own way. Many have received the Saviour into their lives, and are completely changed. Many former addicts are now working for the Lord and reaching out to those who are in the same state as they once were. They will testify to the fact that Christ is the answer to drug addiction, and indeed, to every other problem in life.

There are important signposts pointing to the near return of Christ, and I will list some of them:

1. The increase of international revolution.
2. The increase of wars and rumours of war.
3. The increase of famines.
4. The increase of knowledge.
5. The increase of earthquakes.
6. The flood of occultism and false cults.
7. The move towards a one-world religion.
8. The departure of some of the churches from the historic truths of Christianity.
9. The increase of lawlessness.
10. The increase of suicides.
11. Men's hearts failing them for fear because of the increase of wickedness.
12. The apathy of people because of hardship; unemployment being just one example.

It is not my intention to go into great detail about the events following the rapture of the church. This is another study of its own, and many books have been written on the second coming of Christ, and what follows it. Sad to say, there has also been a lot of controversy and even heated arguments as to whether the rapture will take place before the great tribulation or half-way through, or whether we are in fact in the tribulation right now. While there are debates and arguments and speculation about this and about the anti-christ, the most important point is being missed. God will fulfil all that is written in the Scriptures. Everything will take place precisely as God has planned it. In His exact time, and in His exact order.

Every Christian knows that these things will happen. We know in advance what Satan's end will be, so it's pointless to speculate and argue. This is just what the devil wants people to do. Instead, we should be busy proclaiming the gospel story, warning of the near coming of the Lord Jesus Christ, and pointing lost souls to Christ who is the only escape from the things that are going to happen upon the earth. Our task is to keep our eyes on Jesus and to be obedient to His word, and walk in His ways.

There is evidence that Satan knows his is a lost cause, but this does not mean he will slacken his efforts to wrest victory from his approaching doom. Indeed, he will pour more and more wickedness, more and more deception into our generation. We must keep courage and faith as the distress increases, knowing that one thing is certain—God and His righteousness shall triumph; the devil cannot win. To bring this chapter to a close, I would like to share with you a poem I wrote some time ago which puts what I have been saying into a nutshell.

The day of his appearing

When we read the daily papers and listen to the
   news,
Then we read what the Bible has to say,
Events we see and hear about are foretold in God's
   word,
They are signposts to the coming judgment day,
We are living in the latter days, there is trouble
   everywhere,
With earthquakes, false prophets, division and
   war,
Men's hearts are failing them for fear on every
   hand,
As wickedness increases more and more.

Evil signs and lying wonders, and scoffers all
   around,
Blasphemers, who God's Holy word deny,

Dark powers will soon be shaken, sun and moon
   will cease to shine,
All the stars will be falling from the sky,
Then a far greater light will be seen in this dark
   world,
When the Son of Man in power and glory comes,
With a host of holy angels, in a radiancy so bright,
It will outshine a thousand billion suns.

There is no condemnation for the blood-bought
   child of God,
No fear of punishment, no death, no pain,
We are looking for that blessed hope when Jesus
   we shall see,
Then forever with our Saviour we shall reign,
For we shall be changed in a twinkling of an eye,
When we rise up to meet Him in the air,
Receive a crown of glory that fadeth not away,
In the City of our God bright and fair.

As in the days of Noah just before the mighty flood,
Men continue in rebellion just the same,
All those outside the ark of salvation will be lost,
Very soon the Lord will shut the door again.
So let us be as watchmen, and warn them of the
   night,
Let us raise up our banner—hold it high,
Lift up our voice like a trumpet—shout aloud,
The coming of the Lord is drawing nigh.

CHAPTER TEN

The four keys of authority

WHEN we look at the life of Christ, there can be no doubt that He knew who He was. He knew He was the Son of God. He knew he was King. He knew why He had come to earth. He knew he had power and authority. He was never stumped for an answer, and He was in perfect harmony with His Father's time-table; ''Father, the time has come. Glorify your Son, that your Son may glorify you'' (Jn 17:1).

There are two kingdoms, one of darkness, the other of light; one is ruled by Satan, the other by God. The kingdom of God is far more powerful than the king-dom of darkness. Christ manifested kingdom living while He was dwelling on this earth. He was con-stantly in communion with His Father, and speaking about His Father's kingdom.

Kingdom living is only possible through the cross. The kingdom of God is born in us through the cross when we repent and turn from our sin. When Jesus started His ministry, Satan knew that the kingdom of God was advancing and his dark kingdom was in jeop-ardy. Our work today is to extend the kingdom of God. What Jesus accomplished on Calvary, we can carry on doing through the power of the Holy Spirit within us. The life of Christ was repeated by His dis-ciples and the early church. The power of the Holy Spirit enabled them to do what Jesus did.

Where there is a kingdom, there is a king who rules and reigns. Jesus Christ is the King of Kings and Lord of Lords. He is reigning in our hearts, and we can experience kingdom rule and reign with Him: "The kingdom of God is within you" (Lk 17:21). It is a spiritual kingdom. God gives us grace to live as sons and daughters, to rule and reign in life. All the fullness of God dwelt in Jesus Christ, and we can know the fullness of God in our lives, just as Jesus did, for we read in Ephesians 3:19, "That you may be filled to the measure of all the fullness of God."

We have authority to reign with Him, for He has given us the keys of the kingdom. We belong to the household of God and we reign as kings and priests, right now! 1 Peter 2:9 tells us, "But you are a chosen people, a royal priesthood, a holy nation, a people belonging to God, that you may declare the praises of him who called you out of darkness into his wonderful light." The question is, as children of His wonderful kingdom and wonderful light and as children of a King, are we living as kings and priests, as He wants us to? Are we claiming our inheritance? We can reign with Him in every situation, conquer every foe, have victory in trouble and temptation, and power over all the power of the devil. Jesus reigned in life, meeting every need, and we can do the same. The laws of the kingdom are written in our hearts. The laws of the kingdom are found in God's word. "I will put my laws in their minds and write them on their hearts. I will be their God, and they will be my people" (Heb 8:10).

Jesus said this, "In my Father's house there are many rooms; if it were not so, I would have told you. I am going there to prepare a *place* for you" (Jn 14:2). Many people picture this as a place where angels sing and play harps, and where we will all go sometime in the future. Jesus went to prepare a *place* for us now, as well as in the future: a *place* of blessing for us, a *place* of victory and authority, and power over all the power of the devil, day by day. I have seen this even more as I have come across the demons who have opposed me, and the ministry the Lord has given me, and when I have been used in casting out demons from those who have been demon possessed and oppressed. He gave me a place of victory to do what was needed in the hour of need.

This is what we read in Ephesians 2:6, "And God raised us up with Christ and seated us with him in the heavenly realms in Christ Jesus." We can experience blessing and victory now, because we are seated with Him in the heavenly realm, in the place of authority, and the devil is under our feet. When the devil knows that I recognise who I am in Christ, he does not bother with me, in fact, he is afraid of me. Many people I have met have told me plainly, "I am afraid of the devil," others do not actually state they are afraid of him, but I know they are, and cannot understand why I am not fearful of him. In fact, I have been asked, "Doreen, how is it that you are not afraid of the devil?" My answer was, "Why should I be?" "Well, you were in his grasp for so long" they replied. "Yes, that is true, but I am not now, am I? I belong to the Lord Jesus Christ, and He has given me authority over him, in His name. The devil is afraid of me now, because Jesus in me is greater than him, and all the hosts of hell put together."

Christians have not recognised their place as conquerors in Christ. This is sad, and I wondered why at first, but now I realise that many do not receive the right teaching, and some have not grown in the Lord or read and believed His word.

The authority of His name

Jesus has a name higher than any other name. It is higher than Gabriel, it is higher than the name of any earthly potentate. "Therefore God exalted him to the highest place and gave him the name that is above every name, that at the name of Jesus every knee should bow, in heaven and on earth and under the earth, and every tongue confess that Jesus Christ is Lord, to the glory of God the Father" (Php 2:9–11).

In this spiritual kingdom where we are reigning with Christ, He has given us keys, and the name of Jesus is one of them. He has placed this key in our hands and He wants us to use it. In Exodus 4:1–4, the Lord tells Moses to throw his staff upon the ground; he did so, and it became a snake. The Lord then told him to reach out his hand and take it by the tail. Moses reached out, took hold of the snake, and it turned back into a staff in his hand. He later used the staff to part the Red Sea. A staff represents a rod of authority. What the staff was to Moses, the name of Jesus was to the apostles.

In 1 Samuel 17:45 we read that David said to the Philistine, "You come against me with sword and spear and javelin, but I come against you in the name of the Lord Almighty." David triumphed over the Philistine with a sling and a small stone—without a sword, but with the authority of God. God has given us the authority of the name of Jesus, to come against giants: giants of fear, giants of rebellion, giants of sin and giants of evil. David learned as a lad to trust God. He faced the giant in the name of the Lord, and we can do the same.

Many Christians mumble, "in the name of Jesus" at the end of a prayer, sometimes as an afterthought, but mostly because they have been taught to do so; which is right and good, but using the name of Jesus is an introduction into a personal life in Jesus, not a matter of form and ceremony. The name of Jesus otherwise becomes formal, technical, and of a functional importance only rather than a personal and powerful name. The name of Jesus should not be used parrot-fashion, nor in a flippant way, because His name is precious, so let us use it wisely and with reverence. It would be better still, and be more specific, to give Jesus his full title "The Lord Jesus Christ" because Christ means "the anointed one" as there are many people, even today, named Jesus.

Elijah had a cloak which he used to strike the water and it divided to the right and left, and he crossed over the Jordan (2 Ki 2:8). He used what he had in his hands. In Acts 3:1–10 we read of a man who was crippled from birth. Peter said to him, "Silver or gold I do not have, but what I have I give you. In the name of Jesus Christ of Nazareth, walk'' (verse 6). And he did so. Peter took him by the right hand and he helped him up.

Jesus said in Matthew 28:18-19, ''All authority in heaven and on earth has been given to me. Therefore go and make disciples of all nations, baptising them in the name of the Father and of the Son and of the Holy Spirit.'' Every born-again Christian has the power and authority to tell Satan to go in the name of Jesus. When the seventy-two returned with joy they said, ''Lord, even the demons submit to us in your name.'' Jesus replied, ''I have given you authority to trample on snakes and scorpions and to overcome all the power of the enemy; nothing will harm you'' (Lk 10:17-19).

There are Christians who try to fight the devil blindfolded. If you were a prize boxer, and entered the ring with a blindfold on, you would be beaten to a pulp. The bell rings, your opponent starts punching you, but you can't punch back because you can't see who he is and where he is. You are not fighting your husband, your wife, your children, your pastor or any person of flesh and blood, but a very real foe—Satan. ''For our struggle is not against flesh and blood, but against the rulers, against the authorities, against the powers of this dark world and against the spiritual forces of evil in the heavenly realms'' (Eph 6:12). The trouble with Christians today, and I say this kindly, is that they have too much fear of the devil. Fear is the opposite of faith. The moment you start to fear, the devil has gained a foothold. The door is open for more fears to creep in, and before you know where you are, you are in bondage to fear. The Bible tells us, ''There is no fear in love. But perfect love drives out fear'' (1 Jn 4:18).

The realm of demonic activity is not confined to worldly places. It may be hard to accept the idea of demonic manifestations in a church, but this is the very place where demons are likely to manifest themselves. There is a scriptural precedent for this in Mark 1:23-26: ''Just then a man in their synagogue who was possessed by an evil spirit cried out, 'What do you want with us, Jesus of Nazareth? Have you come to destroy us? I know who you are—the Holy One of God.' 'Be quiet!' said Jesus sternly. 'Come out of him!' The evil spirit shook the man violently and came out of him with a shriek.'' When someone interrupts a service in the house of God, it is more often than not, a demon. The Holy Spirit does not interrupt someone who is preaching under the Holy Spirit's anointing.

One night I was preaching in a tent in Liverpool, when suddenly a man cried out with a loud voice. The whole congregation was silent. They all knew it was a demon by the way he cried out and by his appearance. I silenced the evil spirit in the name of Jesus, and carried on preaching. The evil spirit was quiet until I invited people to come forward for salvation, healing and deliverance. The man came forward, shrieking at the top of his voice. I then commanded the evil spirit to leave in the name of Jesus. The man fell to the floor, the evil spirit came out, and I then led the man to the Lord; he was completely delivered. There was no long dialogue with the demon. There is no need for that. Jesus cast out demons with one word: ''Go''—and the demons left at once. We can cast out demons with six words today: ''Go, in the name of Jesus.'' If demon-possessed people are willing to be freed and are repentant of their sins, demons have to go at once.

The devil is highly delighted with eight-hour deliverance meetings, which last until three in the morning, while demons play hide and seek, wear out the Christians, confound them with knowledge, and frighten them by their strength. It was not like that in the New Testament. Jesus spoke the word and demons came out immediately. The devil has made some Christians believe that casting out demons is a long, hard struggle. This is not true. In fact, it is easier to cast out demons than many people think. The Lord has shown me that his rest enters into the realm of deliverance. It is true that demons come out in various ways. Sometimes they do scream and throw people to the ground. We must not be afraid or astonished should this occur. This should only be a momentary manifestation as the demons leave, not a long, drawn-out process. Prolonged manifestations indicate the need for counselling, repentance and the reading of God's word.

There is a great need for balanced teaching regarding deliverance today, and how to keep it within the body of Christ. Because of unbalanced teaching, which leads to excessive and fanatical demonstrations in the house of God, many have come to the wrong conclusion that demons do not exist. This is a great pity because demon possession, oppression and obsession is increasing as more and more people are involved in the occult and other unclean practices, and many more need deliverance today.

I have been present at a meeting where bowls were provided, into which people could cough up demons; people were going forward and coughing and spitting and there was a lot of shouting and screaming, which caused much confusion. Many got up and left, including me. It is part of the devil's work to make Christians look stupid and bring the gospel of salvation and deliverance from the power of the devil into disrepute. I am not saying that no-one is delivered by such methods, or that they were at fault in any way, but I am saying there is no need and no room for fanatical measures, because they result in the devil getting a lot of glory that is not due to him.

There is not one of us who is exempt from any demonic thought flowing towards us. Many of our temptations are very much the same, for the Scriptures tell us, ''No temptation has seized you except what is common to man. And God is faithful; he will not let you be tempted beyond what you can bear. But when you are tempted, he will also provide a way out so that you can stand up under it'' (1 Co 10:13). There are some people who almost tempt themselves. They begin the day by saying, ''It's not going to be a very good day for me today. I feel depressed. I'm going to have a rotten headache,''—and they are always depressed, and lo and behold, the headache appears. Some people have been in bondage for years over certain areas in their lives. They are always looking on the black side of things and are never positive about anything at all. They have never learned the secret of calling upon the name of Jesus. They have never claimed their inheritance as a child of God. They have never experienced God's power and authority in their lives.

There is a wonderful chorus that was sung frequently at the Billy Graham crusades here in England, called *Majesty*. Some of the lines go like this:

> Majesty, worship His Majesty
> Unto Jesus be glory, honour and praise.
> Majesty, kingdom authority,
> Flow from His throne unto His own,
> His anthem raise.
> So exalt, lift up on high the name of Jesus ...

If we fail to use the key of the name of Jesus, we will be powerless and suffer defeat. The devil does not have to pull out any new tricks for some Christians, because they have fallen for the same trick of the devil for years, and all the devil has to do is to keep it up.

There are four good ways to resist the devil: the first is to quote Scripture, like Jesus did during his forty days and nights in the wilderness. The devil hates the word of God when quoted with authority. It is no use saying in a meek and fearful voice, "Please, Satan, go away," because he won't. If you came home and found someone in your house who was up to no good, you would tell him to leave in no uncertain terms. You must do the same with the devil. You must tell him to go in the name of Jesus, as if you mean it. Using Scripture with power and authority is a sure way to victory over the devil.

A second way is to start praying in the Spirit, namely in the supernatural prayer language of tongues. The devil cannot understand a word of Holy Spirit prayer, so it is impossible for him to eavesdrop for very long, and he will soon leave.

The third way is to learn to be rebellious— rebellious

to Satan. The only time rebellion is accepted by God is when it is rebellion towards Satan. Do exactly the opposite of what he is tempting you to do. For instance, if you are being tempted to say an unkind word, say a kind word instead. If Satan tells you to be bad-tempered, irritable, unhappy and miserable, start singing the praises of the Lord at the top of your voice, if possible. Satan cannot stand to hear God's children singing His praises.

The fourth way to resist the devil is by simply ignoring him and the thoughts that he brings to your mind. I do not believe the Lord went about rebuking the devil all day long. He simply went about His Father's business, listening to His voice and doing His will. "My Father is always at his work to this very day, and I, too, am working" (Jn 5:17). When we learn to ignore the devil we will live in victory in our thought lives.

When the devil can say of us, "I can't even get to talk to him. He just won't listen"—that is victory. That is power and authority over the devil. Many times the devil has tried to tell me something, but as soon as I am aware of it, I simply ignore him. Nothing is more final than silence. We don't have to accept every demonic thought that comes to our minds. Our bodies are temples of the Holy Spirit. I like this Scripture in 2 Corinthians 10:5 which says, "We demolish arguments and every pretension that sets itself up against the knowledge of God, and we take captive every thought to make it obedient to Christ." When we are ruling and reigning in kingdom authority, the effects of sin, seen and manifested all around, cannot possibly affect us, for we are living above these things, seated with Christ in heavenly places.

In John 14:12–13 Jesus tells us, "I tell you the truth, anyone who has faith in me will do what I have been doing. He will do even greater things than these, because I am going to the Father. And I will do whatever you ask in my name, so that the Son may bring glory to the Father."

Behind the name of Jesus is the Godhead. Psalm

138:2 says, "For you have exalted above all things your name and your word." His name represents His will. He wants us to rule and reign. He wants us to use His name. He wants us to learn His secrets. We must ask in faith, speak out in faith, use His name in faith. It is a lovely name, a precious name, a glorious name, a powerful name. "Salvation is found in no-one else, for there is no other name under heaven given to men by which we must be saved" (Ac 4:12).

The key of prayer

The spiritual kingdom that is within us only comes through new birth. We have been born into the kingdom of God through Christ's shed blood on Calvary. There are two kingdoms, one of darkness and one of light: one of Satan and one of God. Light exposes darkness. Light penetrates darkness. Darkness cannot penetrate light. The kingdom of God opposes the kingdom of darkness, and vice versa. The work of Christ's church today is to enforce the victory of Calvary and to continue Christ's mission, which was to destroy the works of the devil (1 Jn 3:8). How? By preaching the gospel, healing the sick, raising the dead and casting out demons, and by taking back the ground that Satan has stolen. Christ conquered the devil at Calvary: "He forgave us all our sins, having cancelled the written code, with its regulations, that was against us and that stood opposed to us; he took it away, nailing it to the cross. And having disarmed the powers and authorities, he made a public spectacle of them, triumphing over them by the cross" (Col 2:13–15).

Satan is violently opposed to those who would come into the kingdom through the cross of Christ. Jesus said we should pray like this: "Your kingdom come." We all know that we will reign on the earth one day in the Millenium, but His kingdom has come now, within our hearts. Jesus went on to say, "Your will be done on earth." It is His will that His kingdom be increased on the earth, and we can put to flight the powers of darkness that would hinder us. It is His will that prisoners should be released; this is why He came. It says in Isaiah 61:1, ''The Spirit of the Sovereign Lord is on me, because the Lord has anointed me to preach good news to the poor. He has sent me to bind up the brokenhearted, to proclaim freedom for the captives and release from darkness for the prisoners.''

Satan has to be bound, and we can do this in prayer. Satan is doing his utmost to stop people from coming to the cross of Christ. The prayers of the blood-washed saints of God can release those whom God is preparing to come into His kingdom. Satan has to yield to the greater power of Jesus Christ. Christ's resurrection shows the extent of His stronger power. His resurrection was victory over death. Christ conquered hell's worst. He took the keys of death and hell away from Satan, and Satan was powerless to stop Him. In James 5:17–18 we read how Elijah prayed earnestly that it would not rain, and it did not rain on the land for three and a half years. He prayed again and the heavens gave rain, and the earth produced its crops. Placed in our hands, prayer is the key to unlock the storehouse of God's provision. It is the key to unlock prison doors for those in darkness and bondage. Prayer opens doors for the impossible. It opens up the way for God to move in and do His work. Prayer prepares the way for the Lord. This key is in our hands, and we can use it. Authority in prayer gives us the ability to communicate with God, to know His mind in matters of utmost importance, and in times of great need in our lives and in the lives of others. We use our voices naturally to communicate and we can use our voices spiritually, our voices can be elevated to speak the things of God. Neglecting to use this key renders us powerless and defeated, and an easy target for the devil to oppress us.

Mark 1:35 tells us that Jesus rose up early in the morning, while it was still dark, to pray. We should begin the day with God in prayer. The ministry of prayer is a very powerful ministry. Revival begins with prayer. Prayer opened up the way of ministry for Jesus to reach out His hand to heal the leper (Mk 1:40–45). The leper recognised the Lordship of Christ. He recognised the authority of Christ. He willingly believed, and submitted to the Lordship of Christ. Submitting to the Lordship of Christ made a way of healing and cleansing.

Prayer does not have to be complicated, long and drawn out, full of complicated, and well thought out sentences. Prayer should be simple, not childish, but asking in childlike faith believing He will hear and answer your prayer. The key of authority is also a key of faith, a simple childlike faith. Jesus gives us the authority to ask: ''I tell you the truth, my Father will give you whatever you ask in my name'' (Jn 16:23). God wants us to be successful, and to get the job done. He is not reluctant to give, or to answer prayer, in fact, I believe it thrills Him to answer our prayers, when we ask according to His will. The barrier is hesitancy, fear, and a reluctance on our part to pray. We must co-operate with God in order to bring His plans and purposes about. God is not so overloaded with requests that He cannot cope with them all. His storehouse is full, we only have to ask. Some Christians do not receive, because they have not asked, or they ask for selfish reasons, which is clearly out of God's will.

Intercessory prayer brings about revelation and illumination of God's plan and purpose. It lights up God's word to us in new ways, and brings revelation in matters of urgency and utmost importance when we engage in it. Yet intercessory prayer is often painful, and it's sacrificial. It means that we have to give of our time to pray, to devote ourselves to prayer, mostly over things of great importance, where we need to know what we must do, and what we should say, and how best to help someone with great difficulty. Words of God's wisdom will be given to us in this kind of praying, not from our own mind, but from the mind of God. God gives us His wisdom, and makes known to

129

us His purposes in prayer. Prayer and fasting is needed when we are going to deliver people from demons, and God will show us His will in this matter. We touch God's throne in intercessory prayer, and this endues us with His strength and power to do what is needed. Are we willing to be taught how to pray? Many are the plans in the heart of man, but it is the Lord's purposes that must prevail. It is no longer what I want, or think I need, it is Him that must increase, and I must decrease. The only way we can know the plan of God for our lives is through prayer, He will show us His plan only when it is His will to do so. If we knew every single thing that He has for our lives, we could well be overwhelmed, for our future is in His hands. It is only when we are going to work for Him, that we need to know His direction. His will for us all is that we should be conformed to the image of His Son (Ro 8:29). As we give ourselves to prayer and His word we will grow to maturity so that we can minister to a lost and dying world. As we give ourselves in full commitment, and make ourselves available to Him, the life of Christ within our hearts will be released to reach out to others who are bound by the devil. This is our spiritual warfare.

The authority of his word

Revelation 1:2 tells us the word of God is the testimony of Jesus Christ. It is also the word of prophecy, and it says in verse 3, ''Blessed is the one who reads the words of this prophecy, and blessed are those who hear it and take to heart what is written in it, because the time is near.'' The disciples were taught by Christ through Old Testament Scriptures. Jesus Christ is the very breath of the testimony of the prophets, for the Old Testament Scriptures were fulfilled in Him. We are a kingdom. ''To him who loves us and has freed us from our sins by his blood, and has made us to be a kingdom and priests to serve his God and Father'' (Rev 1:5-6). Details of how we should serve Him are found in God's word. In Revelation 1:19 John was told to write what he had seen, and what was taking place then, and what would happen in the future—which is now. We can understand what is taking place now by the revelation of the Holy Spirit, and by the written word of God.

If we want Christ to rule in our lives, if we want to experience kingdom rule and reign with Him, we must play our part and obey His word. Jesus said in John 14:21, "Whoever has my commands and obeys them, he is the one who loves me. He who loves me will be loved by my Father, and I too will love him and show myself to him." Jesus will reveal Himself to us as we obey His commands. If we do not obey His commands our victory will be lost. We must put into practice what God is saying. If we want to hear what God is saying, and be blessed by it, we must do as He says. What is the use of hearing His voice, if we do not obey it? How can he bless us if we do not obey His word? There must be a desire in our hearts to hear His voice and obey His word.

There is a restoration today of the teaching ministry, revealing the deep truths of God to us. God speaks to His children through His word, and the gifts of the Holy Spirit.

The prophetic voice is also being heard again today, and we must have open hearts to receive what God is saying to us. When God speaks through prophecy, people with open hearts will understand clearly what God is saying to them. It will give them insight, wisdom and knowledge of the deep truths of God's word, and they will know how to apply it to their lives. The preaching of God's word under the anointing of the Holy Spirit brings about transformation in people's lives. It brings about conversion, healing and release from the grip of Satan. There are many false doctrines going around today, and when we have knowledge of God's word, we can recognise them, and it is important that we do recognise them, or we could be led into error and bondage. If what we hear is not found in God's word, or is twisted in any way, we should shun it completely.

131

His word is eternally settled in heaven, it cannot be altered.

Throughout this book, God's word is being quoted, for without it, this and everything I endeavour to do for God will be of no avail. I love His word, I have come to lean on it more and more. There are many treasures found in His word, many words of comfort, and guidance to steer me through this world. God does not leave us without a light to guide us; how much we need the truth of God's word in a world that is darker than ever before. God's word is a firm foundation to build upon, to go astray from it will lead to the complete collapse of our house, our building. When we build on His word He will bring forth fruit in our lives for the glory of God, which will build up our faith, and bring comfort in times of difficulty and hardship.

The key of the Holy Spirit

In John 2:1–11 we read about the first miracle that Jesus performed, when he turned water into wine at a wedding in Cana in Galilee. They had run out of wine, and nearby stood six stone water jars. Jesus said to the servants, ''Fill the jars with water'' so they filled them to the brim. Then He told them to pour the water, and it turned into wine. The best wine was left to the last.

We are living in the last days today, and God is pouring out the wine of the Holy Spirit upon all flesh. The best wine of the Holy Spirit is kept for this day of visitation. The vessels need to be filled to the brim, not half full, and we, the children of God are the vessels that God wants to fill with the fullness of the Holy Spirit. Holy Spirit prayer, praise and worship will transform us. Holy Spirit praying, preaching, praise and worship in His house prepares the way for the Lord to move in people's hearts. Holy Spirit prayer, praise and worship will create an atmosphere where God can move in and do His work. We must have open hearts to receive what God is doing today. God has difficulty with those who have an independent spirit, because their hearts are closed to what He is doing, and what He wants to do in this world. It is very sad when Christians think they know it all and are unteachable, because they cannot receive what God wants them to receive, a fresh in-filling of His Spirit in their lives, anointing upon their ministry for the Lord. 1 Corinthians 3:9 says, ''For we are God's fellow-workers; you are God's field, God's building.'' He is pouring out the rain of the Holy Spirit upon His people, His field, His building, in order for it to produce fruit.

Our lives are made richer and softer when we allow the Holy Spirit to work in our lives. God wants us to experience a greater outpouring of the Holy Spirit in our lives today. Satan's onslaught on the world is real and very strong, and the Holy Spirit is the only answer, the only way through which we will have power to reach out into the darkness, and pull out of the strong-holds of Satan. Holy Spirit-filled people are the only ones who can be used mightily of God to release the prisoners of darkness. The Holy Spirit will also enable us to rule and reign over circumstances which are against us.

When Paul was in Ephesus, he found some disciples, and asked them if they had received the Holy Spirit when they believed; they answered they had not even heard that there was a Holy Spirit. So Paul asked what baptism they had received, and they replied, ''John's baptism.'' Paul said that John's baptism was a baptism of repentance, and John had told the people to believe in the one coming after him, who was Jesus. When they heard this they were baptised in the name of the Lord Jesus. Paul placed his hands on them, and the Holy Spirit came upon them, and they spoke in tongues and prophesied (Ac 19:1-7). There are still people today who have never heard of the baptism of the Holy Spirit, or the gifts of the Holy Spirit, because in some places it has not been preached. Perhaps some of them have been put off the baptism of the Holy Spirit, because of some of the excesses they have seen, or have heard about. Some do not believe that the baptism of the Holy Spirit is for us today, but just for the birth of the New Testament church. The Bible, however, tells us this, "Repent and be baptised, every one of you, in the name of Jesus Christ for the forgiveness of your sins. And you will receive the gift of the Holy Spirit. The promise is for you and your children and for all who are far off—for all whom the Lord our God will call" (Ac 2:38–39).

We can experience the baptism of the Holy Spirit today, and God is pouring out His Holy Spirit in a mighty way. Miracles are happening today, sick bodies are being healed, the demon possessed are being set free. Those who have been caught up in occult practices, those on drugs, those whose lives have been broken and ruined, are being marvellously delivered and restored.

Preparation for kingdom living was given to us through Christ and the apostles. Kingdom living itself, is just a preparation for the time when we will be living in His presence continually. So it is wise, and also a source of great blessing to get some practice in now. Kingdom living should come naturally, because the kingdom of God dwells within us now. So let us live in victory, confident and joyful, free from fear, worry or stress and strain, so that others will be attracted to us, and we can then talk to them about our Saviour and Lord.

The keys of authority I have mentioned in this chapter are all found in operation in Acts 4:29–31. This was the prayer of the believers: " 'Now, Lord, consider their threats and enable your servants to speak *your word* with great boldness. Stretch our your hand to heal and perform miraculous signs and wonders through the *name* of your holy servant Jesus.' After they had *prayed*, the place where they were meeting was shaken. And they were all filled with *the Holy Spirit* and spoke the word of God boldly." All these keys belong together, although each key has a different function unique in itself. They all work in harmony together, and they are all essential in building up the kingdom of God.

Some time ago I was reading through the book of Nehemiah, that man who had a vision, a burden and a commission from God to rebuild the walls of Jerusalem. The walls of Jerusalem were broken down and the gates were burned with fire. When Nehemiah heard this he mourned and wept, and fasted and prayed before God in heaven. Nehemiah was so sad that it showed on his face, and even the king noticed it asking, "Why does your face look so sad when you are not ill?" Nehemiah answered "Why should my face not look sad when the city where my fathers are buried lies in ruins, and its gates have been destroyed by fire?" (Ne 2:2–3). In other words, Nehemiah said, "I've every right to look sad when my heart is heavy with grief."

Today, when I see the waste places the devil is making in this and other lands: the misery, the pain, the wars, the consequences of sin and godlessness all around me, I can understand how Nehemiah felt. But Nehemiah did not just leave it like that, he did something about it. He had a great burden, and a great vision, and in the end the king himself commissioned him to go and rebuild the broken walls of Jerusalem. While his enemies scoffed, Nehemiah prayed to God and continued with the work God had given him to do. It was no easy task, but he never wavered; he just kept on building up the broken walls and gates. He did not do it alone. The vision of Nehemiah was caught by others, and they helped him in the task God had given him. Everyone involved had a different, important part to play. The high priest rose early in the morning with his brethren to work, and women worked too. There was much to do, and much rubbish had to be cleared away so that the building could begin.

They were well-equipped against the enemy who conspired to hinder the work right from the very beginning. While one half worked, the other half held spears, bows and shields. Some even worked with one hand, and held a weapon in the other, while others blew trumpets to warn of the approaching enemy—these were the watchmen. Every worker held a shield, and they all worked in harmony and unity. How they laboured! From the rising of the sun until the stars appeared at night. How zealous they were in building up the broken walls and gates of Jerusalem!

What we need today are men and women like Nehemiah, with a vision, with a burden, and courage to get on with building up the waste places the devil has made, and is still making in the sin-sick world we live in. We need to rise up in unity and strength, and power to pull down the strongholds of Satan. We need to be men and women with courage, calling and zeal to do what God wants us to do, and to go where He wants us to go.

Oh yes, there will be scoffers, but you will find that the people who scoff do nothing themselves for the Lord. All these people want to do is tear down—but these are the enemies of the Lord, and we should be well equipped against them, just as the watchmen were in Nehemiah's day. The devil is working overtime in diverting, destroying and laying waste precious souls for whom Christ died. We must warn them, we must rescue them before it is too late. We need watchmen who can see with the eyes of faith what is needed to build up the kingdom of God.

We need more men and women of prayer, who can blow away the rubbish that the devil blows in at us, like apathy, unbelief, scoffers, and everyone else who would discourage us from doing the work.

The task of God's children, all of us everywhere, is to create beauty out of the ugliness of this world, and create peace where there is discord and strife. God's children, all of us, should be busy creating love, joy and happier relationships wherever we go. We should be telling people everywhere about the most important and sweetest relationship of all, a personal relationship with the Lord Jesus Christ.

I am glad I read through Nehemiah; because it has helped me. It has enlarged my vision, and encouraged me to go on building up the kingdom of my God. It has helped me to be a better watchman for Him. The hour is getting late. The midnight cry goes out today—will you meet the call? The Lord has given to us, to you and me, the keys of the kingdom, and has given us the authority to bind and loose (Mt 16:19). Will you use those keys?

CHAPTER ELEVEN

The power of love and praise

THE power of love is one of the greatest powers known to men and women. Even those who have never received Jesus as their personal Saviour, know, and have known at some time in their lives, the power of love. The love of a mother for her child is as strong as death, she would willingly lay down her life to save her child. There are all kinds of true stories that have told of the power of human love, where men, women and even children have risked their lives to save another, and have laid down their lives to save people who they have dearly loved. Millions of tears have been shed because of love. Tears of joy, tears of anguish, tears of heart-break and pain have been shed, and still will be, because of love: love of a man for his wife, a wife for her husband, love for parents, love for children, love for brothers and sisters, love for a just cause, love for a country, love for an animal, love for a friend; so powerful is the force of love.

We read in God's word, "God is love." His very nature is love. Love stems from God. Love is a free gift to mankind from God. We read in His word, "How great is the love the father has lavished on us, that we should be called children of God" (1 Jn 3:1). What love can be more merciful, more pure and more kind than the love of Jesus? He loved us even in our sin and shame, and when we cried to Him for mercy, forgiveness, and cleansing, He freely forgave us all. He died that we might be forgiven, restored and healed and free. He never turns anyone away who comes to

Him. Anyone can come to Jesus just as they are, in all their sin and unworthiness, and He takes them into His kingdom of light. What a wonderful Saviour! His love is like a never-ending river that knows no bounds and flows on and on, giving joy and blessing to everyone.

Human love, marvellous though it may be, pales into insignificance compared with His divine love. Human love can be restricted. Its ability to express itself can be limited but the love of God which comes from above is immeasurable. Human love can be debased by lust and deteriorate, or be degraded by jealousy and envy. Many a heart and home has been broken in pursuit of human love, but in God's great love there is no darkness at all. There is no forgetfulness, no unfaithfulness, and no disappointment in God's great love. His love is unfailing. Human love, through disappointments and disloyalty, can turn to hate and bitterness. Some types of love have no vigour or height; they are weak and sickly, they have no power to uplift. The purer love is, the higher it is, and such love always uplifts and never degrades. Restricted love is like a stagnant pool, confined and limited, it cannot flow out.

God's love is liberal and generous. Have you stood beside a waterfall and watched the sunlight play upon the face of the waters as they cascade down? A beautiful sight isn't it! The beauty is the result of the height of its fall. It comes a long way down. That's exactly like the love of Jesus. He came all the way from heaven to earth to show us His love. He came a long way down to pick men and women up. If we want our love to inspire anyone, it must have height and be able to reach down to the deepest depths to lift up, and bring hope to the hopeless, and light in the darkest situation. The love of the Saviour has depth. Jesus stooped low to wash the disciples feet. He sat with publicans and sinners. We read in the Bible that He ''made himself nothing, taking the very nature of a servant, being made in human likeness'' (Php 2:7). God's love can, and does, reach down to the darkest sinner and lifts them up to sit in heavenly places with Christ Jesus. This is what He did for me and you. What a wonderful Saviour!

What has all this got to do with spiritual warfare, you may ask. Plenty, because only the love of Jesus dwelling in us can warn in love those who are in the evil grasp of the devil, and point them to the Saviour. This needs grace, courage, and a great love for lost and sinful mankind. Satan does not want God's children to have compassion for the lost; no! he would frighten us off for fear of what might happen to us if we dare to even try to reach them with the message of God's love.

I well remember how frightened Christians were of me—and I was a Christian! I had received Jesus as my Saviour but they knew about my past and they just could not believe that I was a true Christian. They were also afraid of what they thought was the evil in me; afraid I would somehow contaminate them if they came too near me. It really upset me. I felt rejected by Christians. I used to go away and cry my eyes out and sometimes this rejection frightened me and it really discouraged me. Not for some time did I realise it was the devil, who was by now my enemy as well as theirs, that brought such fear upon them. Christians seemed to be completely devoid of courage, faith and love, and were really frightened of the devil.

Jesus recognised the need for blending opposites. He knew His disciples would face a difficult and hostile world where they would confront evil at its worst. He knew they would meet cold and arrogant men whose hearts had been hardened by the long winter of traditionalism, so he said to them, ''I am sending you out like sheep among wolves.'' He gave to them a formula for action, ''Therefore be as shrewd as snakes and as innocent as doves'' (Mt 10:16).

It is difficult to imagine a single person having, simultaneously, the characteristics of a serpent and a dove, but this is what Jesus expects of us. We must, by His grace, combine the toughness of a serpent and the softness of a dove: a tough mind and a tender heart.

140

Let us consider the need for a tough mind. The tough individual has a strong warrior spirit which makes him able to make decisive judgments and discern truth from falsehood. He is able to make the right decisions at times of utmost importance. He is not chained to conformity, the "we have always done things this way, so why change now?" attitude.

Soft-minded people are afraid to step out in faith for fear of failure and upsetting the crowd. Soft-minded people swallow up everything that looks interesting, from an orange to a tennis ball. The tendency for soft-mindedness is found in man's unbelievable gullibility. Take TV adverts for instance; advertisers have long since learned that most people are soft-minded and they capitalize on this susceptibility with skilful and effective slogans. Few people have the toughness of mind to judge critically and discern the true from the false, fact from fiction. Our minds are constantly invaded by half truths and false information. We must be more mature and strong in our discernment, strong in our decisions in this world of deceit. Soft-minded individuals are prone to embrace all kinds of superstitions. Their minds are constantly invaded by irrational fears, which range from fear of Friday the 13th, to the fear of a black cat crossing their path. The soft-minded man always fears change. He feels security in the status-quo and has a morbid fear of the new. For him the greatest pain is the pain of new ideas, because new ideas involve thinking, and thinking is a pain to him. He wants to freeze the moment, and hold life in the gripping yoke of sameness. Change is too hard; it's a pain for him to have to think things through, it's safer and easier for him to do things on the spur of the moment without thinking of the possible consequences. In the days we are living in there seems to be a universal quest for quick answers and half-baked solutions.

Now let us consider the hard-hearted person. The hard-hearted individual never truly loves. He never experiences the beauty of friendship because he is too cold to feel affection for another and is too self-centred to share another's joy and sorrow. He or she is an isolated island. No outpouring of love links him or her to the mainland of humanity. People can stay on an island of isolation for years, never seeking to reach out, or cry for help, to those who pass by. The hard-hearted person never sees people as people, but rather more like objects or cogs in a wheel. The hard-hearted man depersonalizes life itself. Often these people have had little or no love shown to them. They have never experienced real love so they are unable to show love or express love. The fear of rejection holds many back. Rejection is tragic; it leaves a wound so deep that nothing can cleanse or heal it, except the loving, healing hand of God.

The greatness of our God lies in the fact that He is both tough-minded and tender-hearted. He has qualities of sternness and gentleness. He expresses His toughness in His justice and wrath against wickedness, and His tender-heartedness in His grace, mercy, and compassion. On the one hand God is a God of justice who punished Israel for her waywardness, and on the other hand He is a forgiving Father, whose heart is filled with unspeakable joy when He sees sinners repenting and prodigals returning home. If God were only tough-minded He would be a cold, passionless despot, sitting in some far-off heaven disdaining the human race. If God on the other hand were only soft-hearted, He would be too soft and sentimental to function when things go wrong and would be incapable of controlling what He had made. God is tough enough to transcend the world, and He is tender-hearted enough to live in it. He put on the form of a servant and dwelt among men.

There are times when we need to know that our God is a God of justice. When the lumbering giants of injustice emerge on the earth and cause suffering and pain to untold millions, we need to know that there is a God of swift wrath, who can cut them down and leave them to wither like grass in the sun. When our efforts fail to stop the surging sweep of oppression, we need to know that in this universe there is a God whose matchless strength is a solid contrast to the sordid weaknesses of men.

There are also times when we desperately need to know that our God is a God who possesses compassion and mercy. When we are shattered by the stormy blast that rages around us, when the storms of disappointment threaten to overcome us, we can call upon a tender-hearted God for courage and strength. When our courage fails it is good to know we serve a God who is able to sustain us with His power and might. It is good to know that our God can refill us and refresh us with His tender loving care.

We need the strength to love with a love like God's. Strength to be tough when the situation calls for it, and strength to be humble enough to love the unlovely. God hates sin, but He loves the sinner. He can and He will give us the courage to stand up and be counted among those who stand for righteousness and justice. When we can love with a love like God's, the devil and all his agents will flee from us in fear. My desire is to have the strength to love like Jesus loves, to have the courage to be tough, and to know the gentleness of heart that Jesus has, because: ''You stoop down to make me great'' (2 Sa 22:36).

I have known His tenderness, I have felt His gentleness for me and I have felt with wonder, thrills of holy grace. God's love is as wide as the ocean, deeper than the deepest sea, higher than the highest heaven, and broad enough to encompass the whole human race. God loves witches and satanists! He does not love the sin of witchcraft, He hates it, but all sin is sin and there is no such thing as white lies with God: all lies are lies. God does not put sins into categories labelling one sin worse than another. Rejection of Christ and the way of salvation He offers us, is just as sinful as hatred, pride and jealousy. It is easy to condemn occult practices, but let us be careful not to condemn people. We must remember that God sent His son to die for the whole human race. Let us ask God to fill our hearts with His love for *all* lost and sinful mankind. He came to die for the sins of the whole world. I want to be able to see with the eyes of Christ, love with the heart of Christ, listen with the ears of Christ, lift up with the tender hand of Christ, and be tough with everything that is anti-Christ.

While I have been writing this chapter about the power of love, I have felt the blessing and the love of God welling up within me. Having just read through what I have written, I got so excited I just wanted to go on writing about the love of God because it thrills me so much. I realised that I could never come to an end of speaking about His great and wondrous love. When you begin to meditate on the love of God, speak about the love of God, write about the love of God, a great joy floods your very being, and this leads me naturally and easily into the next section of this chapter.

The power of praise

The purest, sweetest, praise must surely come from a heart that is filled with a tremendous love for God. At these times of blessing, being alone with God, or gathered together with others for prayer, it is easier to praise the Lord. But what about the times when it is not so easy to praise the Lord? I have often been in situations where I have felt far removed from praising God and it is just at these times we should praise the Lord. In the Book of Psalms we read how David praised God in every circumstance. By the very act of praising God his faith was strengthened. He never doubted God had the battle won, even before it commenced. Praise brings faith and faith brings hope; therefore praise, faith and hope will always be intertwined. Faith helps us to accept the divine promises of God in their divine reality; hope goes on to embrace the promises which have already been accepted, and faith is the substance of things hoped for, the evidence of things unseen. When we start to praise the Lord He will honour us, and give us the victory.

David the psalmist shouted the victory against overwhelming odds. He knew God was on his side; he said in Psalm 34:1, "I will extol the Lord at all times; his praise will always be on my lips." When everything and everyone seems to be against us we should start to praise the Lord for the challenge, praise Him for the answers, praise Him for the wisdom he will give us, and He will do the rest. He will not let us down when we honour Him in this way. Remember the disciples of Jesus? They were so discouraged and so fearful because their beloved Master had been crucified and buried. They were gathered behind locked doors for fear of the Jews. At that time they were living on the dark side of the cross, the defeat side of the cross. Many church-goers who have never come to a saving knowledge of His grace are doing just that today—they do not see the Saviour risen, alive, powerful and real. They are dragging around a dead Saviour, and have still got the Lord Jesus nailed to the cross.

Discouragement knocks people flat, and Satan knows it. It is the most powerful tool the enemy has and he uses it to the full. Satan hates to see the child of God on his knees and he hates to see him praising God, so he soon turns tail and runs. I myself was very nearly flattened by discouragement shortly after becoming a Christian, when my fellow Christians avoided me and were afraid of me and could not believe I was a true Christian. "See that," said Satan, "they don't believe you are a Christian, so you may as well give up being one." Satan tried to tell me that I was unwanted by the Christians, therefore God did not want me either. This was a clever trick of the devil, but even though you do not know all the secrets, because you are just a babe in Christ, the Lord knows how to encourage His children and Satan will be put down. No matter how the devil tried to stop me from going on with the Lord, I somehow knew that the Lord did want me and I was indeed a child of God.

Paul must have felt discouraged at times because his past was too fresh in the minds of the Christians of his day, and they did not accept him at first. Through it all Paul went on preaching the gospel and the Lord honoured him with souls. I well remember when I first started to preach the grand-old gospel story: it was in a public house, not a church, and I got more converts than the Christians who went to the church I used to attend. I asked some Christians once, "How many souls have been converted recently?" They looked at me as if I was quite mad. "We do not get many people coming to the church to be saved," they said. "Why?" I wanted to know. "Well, it is not easy to get people saved" they replied. "I preach to people where they are, I go to them, and they do listen, and some do get saved" I replied. I asked the Christians to come with me, and help me, but they were too afraid to come.

So I started to praise the Lord for all the people who would get saved through my ministry on the streets and in the public houses, and the outcome was absolutely amazing—I was leading them to the Lord every single time I went out. I might not have had much encouragement from Christians but the Lord honoured me by giving me souls and it seemed worth all the rejection from my fellow Christians. Praise to God drowns out discouragement and the victory is sure. Listen to what it says in the good news for modern man; these are the words of Jesus Himself: "Blessed are you when people insult you, persecute you and falsely say all kinds of evil against you because of me. Rejoice and be glad because great is your reward in heaven, for in the same way they persecuted the prophets who were before you" (Mt 5:11–12).

If I was able to lead people to the Lord in the public houses and on the streets of Bristol in the early sixties, surely Christians can do the same in the nineties because the Lord has not changed. I believe there will come a time when the gospel will *have* to be preached more on the streets than anywhere else, because this is the place where those who Jesus wants to save will be. Do you realise that more people walk the streets today? More are homeless today, more are roaming the streets as prostitutes today, more young people are unemployed and just drifting around, bored and

146

lonely, with nothing to do and nowhere to go. So what better place to meet them and tell them about the Saviour?

Young Christians, the Lord is looking for you. He knows you can reach people for Himself. He knows they will listen to what you say. Do not let the devil drag them down to hell—go out there and compel them to come into the kingdom of light. Go out there to them, praising the Lord, despite the setbacks. The devil will try to make it look too hard for you; take no notice of him, he is a liar anyway, he cannot tell the truth. Go out in joy and prove for yourselves how faithful and powerful love and praise is. Prove the power of love and praise.

I wish I was still young and strong in health to be able to do street evangelism. I would be out there as often as I could, having the joy of seeing Satan fleeing down the street defeated. Do not be afraid of those who are involved in occult practices, the devil cannot harm you if you belong to Jesus Christ. Jesus is stronger than Satan and sin. The devil is far more afraid of you, so do what the Lord commands: ''Preach the gospel to every creature.'' Do it in the power of the Holy Spirit; do it in great and tender compassion; do it in great joy; do it in boldness.

Do not fear demons, demons cannot harm you either. Remember: ''Greater is He who is in you, than he that is in the world.'' In the name of Jesus, devils fear and fly. The curse of a witch cannot harm you, nothing can harm you. Read, and believe the word of God, and claim the promises of God. Read what the Bible has to say regarding your protection from the power of demons and the authority Jesus has given you over them. Try to memorise these Scriptures as this will be a powerful and effective tool against the lies of the enemy. I have quoted many of these Scriptures throughout this book, see if you can remember them. Fear of demons is only one of the devil's tricks to stop people from reaching out to those who are involved in occult practices, because the devil just does not want

147

them to be delivered and neither does he want you to get powerful in the Holy Spirit for fear he may lose even more of his slaves. When those who have been bound by the devil in occult practices receive the Lord as their Saviour, encourage them in every way. Let them know they are accepted by you, and love them with the love of the Lord. Treat them no differently to anyone else who comes to the Lord because they are no different. God is not a respecter of persons (Ac 10:34).

So young people, go forth in the name of Jesus and meet the needs of the people who are lonely, lost in sin, and bound by the devil. Ask the Lord to fill your heart with compassion for those who are in the darkness. Be filled with the Spirit, go out and slay the giants in the name of Jesus for the Lord is with you and will greatly bless you and give you even more power, even more courage, even more love, even more authority over the devil. Deplete the kingdom of darkness and swell the ranks of the army of the Lord.

CHAPTER TWELVE

The army of the Lord

"**F**INALLY, be strong in the Lord and in his mighty power. Put on the full armour of God so that you can take your stand against the devil's schemes" (Eph 6:10–11).

Does Satan give up on us after we become Christians? Does he leave us alone? No! Satan never gives up; as long as we inhabit these mortal bodies he opposes us. Satan cannot undo our salvation, but he will do his utmost to render us powerless and ineffective as far as spreading the good news of salvation is concerned. He can cause us to grow cold and indifferent toward the things of God, and apathetic about the lost. He can rob us of vision, faith, power and love, if we allow him to.

As Paul concludes his letter to the Ephesians, he depicts the Christian pathway as a struggle, an active fight against Satan and the powers of darkness. As Christians we are called to warfare. Our repentance and faith in Jesus Christ is not the end, it is essentially a struggle against Satan and sin, and the works of evil, some of which you have been reading about in this book. In this fight we are not left to fend for ourselves. The full armour of God is at our disposal, and with this defence we can stand against the wiles of the devil, and anyone and anything the devil uses to oppose us. We are faced with forces of evil today such as have never been known before. We are not in civvy street, we cannot take our boots off, and rest on our laurels: we are in the army, God's army, and the Lord wants us to work together with Him, so that the army will grow, both in numbers and in His strength and power.

We are instructed to be strong in God's mighty power by putting on the full armour of God (not just part of it). The devil has weapons which he uses against the children of God, and we too need weapons, and we have them, and the authority to use them. We are soldiers of the cross, soldiers of Christ the King, we belong to the army of the Lord. And the Lord's army is far greater and stronger than the army of Satan. Jesus, who is the author of our salvation, is also our Captain, and He goes before us. The battle is the Lord's, He fights for us and with us, and we must keep our eyes on Him (Heb 12:2).

Paul was often in prison, often in chains (2 Co 11:23) which gave him time to take in every part of the Roman soldier's dress. He would have been able to give an accurate description of the armour, and this probably inspired him to write Ephesians 6:10–18, giving us a spiritual picture of the armour of God, and how to fight the good fight of faith which he mentions in 1 Timothy 6:12 and 2 Timothy 4:7.

In an army every soldier is properly equipped for battle, and trained for warfare, or they would be cut down on the battlefield. They are taught how to use their weapons, and are expected to be well-disciplined and obedient to their superiors. As soldiers of Christ we should be the same. It is only those who are obedient to Him, and walk in His ways, who will be victorious. We must obey Him in every area of our lives: ''Whoever has my commands and obeys them, he is the one who loves me'' (Jn 14:21). God has set His leaders in His army and we must submit to their authority, for it comes from God (Heb 13:17). There are many today who will not submit to the leadership which God has placed in His house: they would rather do their own thing, and go their own way. Is it any wonder that so many are so easily led astray, and fall into deception and error?

We are instructed to endure hardship as good soldiers

of Christ Jesus, and not be influenced by the opinions of those who are not in the army of the Lord. "It is better to trust in the Lord than to put confidence in man" (Ps 118:8 AV). A good example is set us in 2 Timothy 2:3–5 and in Hebrews 12:7–12. It may seem hard, but it produces results, it produces fruit, and it is for our good.

As true soldiers of Christ we are instructed to put on the full armour—literally the panoply of God. Paul urges us to an awareness of the nature of the fight, he warns us against the wiles of the devil (Eph 6:11) and urges us to know his strategy. Satan is a very subtle foe and works and plots, not openly, but by stealth and cunning behind the scenes. It is not a fight against flesh and blood, but against the rulers, against the authorities, against the powers of this dark world, and against the spiritual forces of evil in the heavenly realms. The principalities and powers of which Paul speaks in Ephesians 6:12 appear to be beings and forces that originated in creation (Col 1:16), but now stand against God. These are coupled with the world rulers of darkness who, according to the book of Daniel, appear to be demonic forces who control the evil ambitions of nations and rulers in an attempt to undermine the will of God. Great wickedness is not the result of a badly adjusted society, or the petty failings of a few individuals at the top. There is a mighty force of evil trying to govern a world system against the will of God.

If we minimise the power of the devil or of evil, we do so at our own risk. The enemy is spiritual, the foe we face today attacks minds, bodies and spirits. His sphere of operation is described as being in "high places" literally, "heavenly places". He attacks the place to which the sinner has been raised by the quickening effects of salvation. Ephesians 2:6 says: "God raised us up with Christ and seated us with him in the heavenly realms in Christ Jesus." Satan wants to bring us down, to seek to poison our sanctification, to damage our faith, to block the process of holiness, to penetrate the realm of our thoughts, and to pervert the very high calling of

God. This is the enemy, and this is spiritual wickedness in high places.

The enemy is very real, and the effects of his activities are very real and often devastating. He seeks to enter each day to insinuate his purpose into our very thoughts and actions. Never underestimate him, for to do so would mean that we lack awareness both of the nature of the fight against Satan, and the forces of darkness with which we contend.

The first, and perhaps the most important part of the armour of God is the helmet of salvation. First of all you must be born again by the Spirit of God: "Clothe yourselves with the Lord Jesus Christ" (Ro 13:14); "Put on the new self" (Eph 4:24). The "new self" is the regenerated person as distinguished from the "old self" (Ro 6:6), and is a new person in having become a partaker of Christ's divine nature and life (Col 3:3–4). In no sense is the "old self" improved in any way. "Therefore, if anyone is in Christ, he is a new creation; the old has gone, the new has come!" (2 Co 5:17). The "new self" is Christ, "formed" in the Christian. "For it is by grace you have been saved, through faith—and this is not from yourselves, it is the gift of God—not by works, so that no-one can boast" (Eph 2:8–9). Christ is our salvation.

We must understand what wearing the helmet of salvation means. We know salvation, or deliverance from the *penalty* of sin, as we accept Christ as our personal Saviour. We can know salvation, or deliverance from the *power* of sin, as we continue to follow Him and obey His commands. I like what it says in John 1:12 (AV): "But as many as received him, to them gave he *power* to become the sons of God, even to them that believe on his name." As we wear this helmet daily, we shall know salvation from the *presence* of sin in the future, when the Church Militant becomes the Church Triumphant at the second coming of Christ—the hope of our salvation. Exciting, isn't it?

Furthermore, the constant wearing of the helmet of salvation is a protection from the onslaughts of Satan to the mind. God's word tells us to, "Be transformed by the renewing of your mind" (Ro 12:2). How do we do this? By reading God's word, by believing God's word, and by putting it into practice. In Isaiah 26:3 we read, "You will keep in perfect peace him whose mind is steadfast, because he trusts in you." God also gives us a sound mind (2 Ti 1:7 AV). There is often a battle in the mind. Satan is clever, he knows the mind is the greatest battlefield, and he can have a field day if you let him. Christians have said to me while I have been counselling them, "I can't help it; sinful thoughts keep coming to my mind." I have replied, "We may not be able to stop wrong thoughts coming to our minds, but we can choose what to do with them after they get there." There is an old saying which is so true, "You can't stop the birds flying over your head, but you can stop them from building a nest in your hair." If we harbour wrong thoughts instead of taking authority over them in the name of Jesus, it will cause much spiritual bondage. We do not have to allow our minds to be used like an open field, so that the devil can trample across it, and use it as a dustbin. We do not have to be governed by sinful thoughts. In God's word we read, "We demolish arguments and every pretension that sets itself up against the knowledge of God, and we take captive every thought to make it obedient to Christ" (2 Co 10:5).

Wearing the helmet of salvation we enjoy spiritual blessing in Christ: "Praise be to the God and Father of our Lord Jesus Christ, who has blessed us in the heavenly realms with every spiritual blessing in Christ" (Eph 1:3). So let us enjoy our salvation, live out our salvation to the full, sing about our salvation, talk about our salvation! Then we will experience the reality of Philippians 4:6–7: "Do not be anxious about anything, but in everything, by prayer and petition with thanksgiving, present your requests to God. And the peace of God, which transcends all understanding, will guard your hearts and your minds in Christ Jesus."

Working from the head downwards, the next piece of

the armour of God is the breastplate of righteousness. When we experience salvation, we start to walk a new pathway. Jesus, our Captain, is also the Good Shepherd, and guides us in the paths of righteousness (Ps 23:3). Christ is our righteousness. We have no righteousness of our own, but He gives us His righteousness. As we are obedient to Him and follow Him, this righteousness will increase in us. The righteousness which Paul speaks of in Ephesians 6:14 is not the righteousness that Christ imputes to us, but the practice of righteousness, the character of the believer, which springs up from the righteousness that Christ imputes to us as believers. We must put on righteousness, as a deliberate act, in obedience to God's word. Doing what is right and pleasing to God, and avoiding that which is not righteous, will give us sure victory over the devil, and it will be a testimony to those who are lost. Righteousness is another part of the protective armour of God.

The next part of the armour is the belt of truth. In Paul's day the belt was the symbol of the Roman soldier. The girding up of the loins, the gathering up of the garment under the belt, was a prelude to marching, and indeed fighting. The soldier was made more mobile, and naturally more effective. We, as Christ's soldiers, must don the belt of truth as an act of obedience. We must always speak the truth, and hate all lies and deceit, cast away all that is false and untrue, which would cause us to fall on the battlefield. We cannot be hindered by dishonesty, disloyalty, or deceit as true soldiers of the cross. Jesus is all truth; He is the way, the *truth* and the life, and He will lead us into all truth. It gives God great joy to see His children walking in the truth, because this means we are being conformed to the likeness of His Son. The devil is a liar and the father of lies. He is delighted when God's children resort to lies and deceit, and will entice them into further falsehoods and keep them defeated. So it is of vital importance for Christian soldiers to surround themselves with the truth at all times. Truth is found in

God's word; His word is true from the beginning, so let us please His great heart of love and walk in the light of truth, and put Satan to flight.

Paul speaks of our feet being shod "with the preparation of the gospel of peace" (Eph 6:15 AV). In Paul's time, gall traps, or sharp sticks, were set into the ground to impede the progress of approaching armies, so the feet of the Roman soldier needed to be well shod to surmount these obstacles. We too, by constant renewal in the gospel of Jesus Christ, must be ready and alert. There must be preparation of the heart and mind in order to bring the good news of the gospel to those who are lost. We must be prepared to go where He wants us to go, and do what He wants us to do. Let us also be aware of the obstacles that Satan would place in our pathway to try to stop us from doing this, and then we can march forward sure-footed to victory.

The Christian soldier is now clothed from head to foot in the full armour of God, but three other vital elements are needed: the shield of faith, the sword of the Spirit, which is the word of God, and prayer in the Spirit. The Roman shield, which was made of wood and then covered in leather, was large enough to protect the whole body. In ancient warfare, missiles, first dipped in tar and then ignited, were hurled through the air at the advancing army, which was why Paul used the expression "flaming arrows". The shield not only protected the Roman soldier by stopping the flaming arrows, but actually extinguished their flames, making them totally harmless.

The shield of faith performs the same function for the Christian soldier. With faith as our protection we can render all the flaming arrows of opposition, fear, doubt and anything else the enemy would hurl at us, completely harmless and useless. Satan will endeavour to shake our faith and confidence in our God, in His love for us, in His word, His protection, His power, His faithfulness, His mercy and grace. He often uses human circumstances in order to do this, and we must be aware of his sinister schemes. We must hold up the shield of faith, by putting our complete trust in our God, for He is faithful. He is mighty and strong; He never fails us even though we at times may fail Him. He remains faithful and true forever; he cannot break His word. The Bible gives numerous accounts of how God rewarded His servants who put their complete trust in Him. Even though everything else was against them, God never let them down once, and neither will He let us down. In Hebrews 11:6 we read: ''Without faith it is impossible to please God.'' But with God nothing is impossible. Faith in God is a mighty weapon against the enemy of our souls, so let us use it. Let us put it into operation so that God will reward us, and Satan will flee.

No soldier is properly equipped without his sword. The shield protected the Roman soldier, but his sword slew the enemy and eliminated him altogether. We can do the same with the sword of the Spirit, which is the word of God. We can slay the enemy of our souls with the word of God. Satan hates God's word, because God's word is infallible. The integrity of the word is the basis of faith, so faith and God's word always go together. The reason for unbelief and a faltering faith is a lack of assurance of the integrity of the promises in the word of God. In Romans 10:8 it is called, ''the word of faith.'' God's word gives birth to faith; it is God's faith expressed. Hebrews 11:3 states: ''By faith we understand that the universe was formed at God's command, so that what is seen was not made out of what was visible.'' All God did to create was to say, ''Let there be,'' and there leapt into being the things that are. God and His word are one. He named Jesus ''the Word'': ''In the beginning was the Word, and the Word was with God, and the Word was God. He was with God in the beginning. Through him all things were made; without him nothing was made that has been made'' (Jn 1:1–3). God linked Himself with His word. He made Himself part of it, and you cannot separate Him from His word.

In Genesis 22:16–17 we read this: ''I swear by myself . . .

I will surely bless you and make your descendants as numerous as the stars in the sky and as the sand on the seashore." This was God's promise that backed the Abrahamic Covenant. Abraham believed just what was spoken to him. He did not waver through unbelief regarding the promise of God, but was strengthened in his faith, being fully persuaded that God had power to do what He had promised.

All heaven is behind God's word and backs up God's word. The very throne of God is behind God's word and Jesus and the Father are behind the throne. They are all a part of this word, and he watches over His word to fulfil its promises for, "He cannot deny himself" (2 Ti 2:13 AV).

In 1 Thessalonians 2:13 Paul thanked God that the people received his words as the word of God: "And we also thank God continually because, when you received the word of God, which you heard from us, you accepted it not as the word of men, but as it actually is, the word of God, which is at work in you who believe." The word of God is active; it is always for now, it is never old, it is always fresh and new. The word of God is like its author: eternal, unchanging, living. "The word of God is living and active. Sharper than any double-edged sword, it penetrates even to dividing soul and spirit, joints and marrow; it judges the thoughts and attitudes of the heart" (Heb 4:12). Now notice the next verse: "Nothing in all creation is hidden from God's sight. Everything is uncovered and laid bare before the eyes of him to whom we must give account." Of what is he speaking? He is speaking of the living Word, Jesus, who is the Word!

The Father's word in the mouth of Jesus accomplished things. It stilled the storm; it quietened the wind; it healed the sick, cast out demons, raised the dead and fed the multitudes. His living word on our lips today can do the same thing. When you know, without a shadow of doubt that the Word of God is speaking, you will speak the word with authority. Remember, that faith in God is faith in His word. The senses war against the recreated spirit holding it in bondage, refusing to act on the word, and until the mind is renewed, the word will never have its proper place in the believer's life. Reason must give place to the word of God, for reason often robs the word of God of its authority. When you know that His word is as authoritative today as it was when it fell from the lips of Jesus, then the word will be a living reality in you.

Let the word of God dwell in you richly. Start to confess the word. Hide God's word in your heart. Meditate upon His word and let it grow in you. Stand upon His word. Act upon His word. His word is a living message to us now. The reality of His word flowing through us, throbbing in us, is real; it is the foundation for faith, and faith gives substance to prayer, and makes prayer a reality. It gives us boldness to enter the holy place. What a mighty sword! What a deadly weapon it is to Satan! Soldiers of Christ, use your swords, come against the enemy with it, cut down the forces of evil in His name.

We are surrounded by demonic forces that are dominating the earth, and if the church hasn't authority over these, then no-one has. But the church has, and prayer is its method of dominating these forces. Everyone has a place in the prayer life; God has no inferior sons and daughters. There is no useless member in the physical body and neither is there in the spiritual body. God has planned the body of Christ with infinite wisdom, and the moment you are born again by the Spirit of God you have a place in which to function. So take your place, give yourself to prayer and meditation, and the study of God's word. Don't allow anything to stand in the way of finding your place.

No-one can say that they have no responsibility in the prayer life. To see a need, whatever it is, is a call to prayer. There is much need, in our homes, in our schools, in our places of business, in our church, in our nation. There is breakdown in homes, in business, and in spiritual life, because of the absence of intercessory prayer. If you are a wife, a mother, or a husband, there are certain duties which you perform every day for your family. The greatest duty that you can perform will be prayer duty. Paul says, "Pray in the Spirit on all occasions with all kinds of prayers and requests. With this in mind, be alert and always keep on praying for all the saints (Eph 6:18).

Prayer has several elements. It brings you into contact with the Father, and with the Holy Spirit, and with Jesus. All three members of the Godhead are brought into the prayer life. You are praying *to the Father*. You are praying *in the name of Jesus*. You are praying *through the power of the Holy Spirit*. It brings our hearts into contact with the heavenly centre of all divine power. It is possible to spend any length of time in prayer without being affected by it.

In the very beginning the first man, Adam, lived in the presence of the Creator, his Father. He had no sense of inferiority, no sense of fear or guilt, for he belonged, and because he belonged he took his place as a child of God. Then in one foolish moment he sold out all his vast privileges and rights to the enemy, Satan, and was driven away from the presence of God. God then made a covenant with Abraham, giving him a promise of the Messiah to come through his seed. His descendants were also given a Law and a priesthood; the covenant was made with Jehovah through the priest. God dwelt in their midst in the Holy of Holies. No-one could approach Him unless he was covered by a cloud of incense, and had a basin of blood in his hand to sprinkle on the mercy seat, and that could only be done once a year by the appointed priest.

Down through all history, people's hearts have hungered for true worship and true fellowship with the true God. Satan sets up all kinds of diversions, all kinds of perverted worship. The incarnation of Jesus, the birth of Christ into this dark world of sin, was God's master-stroke of love for lost, fallen, deluded mankind. In His life on earth, Jesus talked with God His Father, the God of the Jews, with an intimacy that they could not understand. He called their God His Father. They

159

took up stones to stone Him for it. They accused Him of blasphemy for it. They crucified Him for it. Jesus paid the price of confessing that God was His Father.

Before Jesus died He said, "I am the way and the truth and the life. No-one comes to the Father except through me" (Jn 14:6). Later on, Paul, who was then Saul, was sent to Damascus with authority to arrest any that he found who were of "the Way" (Ac 9:2). There are several other references in Acts to Christianity as "the Way". In his trial, Paul, defending himself, said, "I admit that I worship the God of our fathers as a follower of the Way" (Ac 24:14). Why did he call it "the Way" and preach that Christ was the "Way" into God's presence? Hebrews 10:19-22 makes it clearer: "We have confidence to enter the Most Holy Place by the blood of Jesus, by a new and living way." Jesus, our great High Priest, was the way into the presence of the Father. We can now draw near with sincere hearts in full assurance of faith. We can now understand Mark 15:38, "The curtain of the temple was torn in two from top to bottom."

The sin problem has been settled because Christ was made sin for us, that we might be brought into full fellowship with the Father. God can be approached, he can be met. Why do His children neglect to meet Him in prayer? Adam lost the way, but what Adam lost has now been restored through Christ's death upon the cross, and there is now a restored righteousness, a restored fellowship. When you grasp what this means, you will grasp the meaning of prayer. It means we can stand in the Father's presence without a sense of guilt, condemnation, or inferiority. The last barrier between the Father and His children has been removed for us by Christ, and we can come into His presence with the same freedom that Jesus had. Prayer is not the old idea of pleading, begging, and crying. We can come to the throne of grace with boldness, with confidence, so we may "find grace to help us in our time of need" (Heb 4:16). We stand in God's presence with fullness of joy, fullness of fellowship, fullness of love.

Relationship means nothing without fellowship. Fellowship means "drinking out of the same cup." The Father has called us into communion with His Son; we drink together. We come with the fruit of our lips, our praise and worship. Our prayers are the fruit of the vine. Jesus said of Himself, "I am the vine; you are the branches. If a man remains in me and I in him, he will bear much fruit" (Jn 15:5).

We come into God's presence with thanksgiving. We come with our praise, we come with our love, we come with our heartaches and burdens, and we come with our petitions. Jesus wants us to come, and He also wants us to ask. These are the words of Jesus: "Until now you have not asked for anything in my name. Ask and you will receive," and note his next words, "and your joy will be complete" (Jn 16:24). It says in James 4:2–3 that we do not have because we do not ask, or we ask with the wrong motives. I like what it says in Ephesians 3:20–21; "Now to him who is able to do immeasurably more than all we ask or imagine, according to his power that is at work within us, to him be glory in the church and in Christ Jesus throughout all generations, for ever and ever! Amen." Nothing can take the place of prayer. How desperately we need it! How desperately the church needs it! No wonder Paul said, "Pray in the Spirit on all occasions" (Eph 6:18).

The armour of God is held together with prayer. It is an armour of light. "The night is nearly over; the day is almost here. So let us put aside the deeds of darkness and put on the armour of light" (Ro 13:12). We are children of the light: "You are all sons of the light and sons of the day. We do not belong to the night or to the darkness" (1 Th 5:5). Now notice verse eight, "But since we belong to the day, let us be self-controlled, putting on faith and love as a breastplate, and the hope of salvation as a helmet."

If you can just catch a glimpse, a vision, of the army of the Lord, all marching forward to victory, all clad in the full armour of God, which is an armour of light, picture how great that light would be! Now place yourself in that army, and hear the mighty sound of it. It is the sound of praise, the sound of war, the sound of victory. What an army! When you put yourself in that army there will be no place for the devil, no place for fear, for you will live in victory over all the power of the devil. You will be assured that the devil is a defeated foe—he cannot win. Furthermore, not only is the army of blood-washed saints bigger and greater than the devil's host, but God has a vast army of angels too, and they are on our side. Listen to what it says in Psalm 68:17 AV: "The chariots of God are twenty thousand, even thousands of angels: the Lord is among them, as in Sinai, in the holy place." Tremendous, isn't it? We also read in Hebrews 12:22: "But you have come to Mount Zion, to the heavenly Jerusalem, the city of the living God. You have come to thousands upon thousands of angels in joyful assembly." What a great and might army! What a privilege it is to belong to it, to be part of it! Praise the Lord!

There is a shout of victory in the camp because, "The angel of the Lord encamps around those who fear him, and he delivers them" (Ps 34:7). Whatever the devil is doing today, there is still much he cannot do, much he cannot stop. He cannot stop the kingdom of God from increasing and advancing. "From the days of John the Baptist until now, the kingdom of heaven has been forcefully advancing, and forceful men lay hold of it" (Mt 11:12). Satan cannot stop the building of Christ's church, His army, and Jesus Himself said, "I will build my church, and the gates of Hades will not overcome it" (Mt 16:18).

Jesus has equipped His church with keys and with weapons to use against the devil. "The weapons we fight with are not the weapons of the world. On the contrary, they have divine power to demolish strongholds" (2 Co 10:4). Christ is returning for a victorious church, not a defeated one. Christ is returning for a radiant church: "Christ loved the church and gave himself up for her to make her holy, cleansing her by the washing with water through the word, and to present her to himself as a radiant church, without stain or wrinkle or any other blemish, but holy and blameless'' (Eph 5:25–27). To Him be all the praise and glory for evermore!

I have come to the end of this book. The mystery of iniquity has been revealed, but more important still, so has the way of deliverance; so has the way of restoration; so has the way of victory; so has the way of overcoming iniquity through Christ the risen Lord, so:

> Soldiers of Christ arise,
> And put your armour on,
> Strong in the strength which God supplies
> Through his eternal Son.
>
> From strength to strength go on,
> Wrestle and fight, and pray;
> Tread all the powers of darkness down,
> And win the well fought day.